# You Can Have It All

(Book 3 in The Hope Book Series)
by Dr. Dene Eller
(Introduction by Serena Carcasole)

Anastasia Bezugla, Carina Cheng Casuga, Cathy Domoney,
Dr. Angelica Benavides, Dr. Emily L. Cross, Heidi Albarbary
Lena Thompson, Michele Duhigg, Marion Segree,
Petra Buric, Samantha Touchais, Sonia Michelle Reynolds,
Tamika L. Blythers, Vanessa Zamora

# Dedication

This book is warmly dedicated to Coach Joyce Wilhelm—a consistently positive, caring adult who served as a beacon of light in my life during very dark times. Not only did Coach improve my sports skills, but she also instilled in me valuable lessons that shaped my "go-for-my-best" disposition forever. As I grew older and followed a similar career path by teaching and coaching others to success, I came to realize that Coach's never-give-up encouragement and belief in me served as an anchoring of confidence in all my life pursuits. Many times before her passing, I fondly remembered her locker room pep talks and her genuine love of serving others. Her light continues to glow in my heart as I pass forward those lessons to others. 'COACH' lives forever

Dr. Dene Eller

# Contents

Self-Image Dictates Your Environment and Results
By Petra Buric
............................................................................101
The AWE Network

# Introduction

## Serena Carcasole

President, Amazing Women Media, Inc.

Dear Reader,

If you're here, chances are you're searching for something.

You want more from your life, right? And although you aren't sure how to get it, you have an inner knowing that it *is* possible (or at the very least, worth a try!).

If you're simply surviving, or just getting by, I want you to know that there is more for you in this life ... IF you're willing to commit to cultivating the right mindset and taking action ... while trusting that the universe has your back and will provide for you.

My mission, through the empowering, inspiring stories within the pages of this book, is to prove to you that you CAN have it all.

Your mind is the most powerful tool you have for achieving your dreams.

Take, for example, the story of lead author Dene Eller. She overcame the effects of a painful, violence-filled childhood and ignited a fire within herself to create a life she absolutely loved— one in which she feels she truly has it all. Now, she's known as "Dr. SUCCESS coach," and her mission is to empower others to reach peak performance. She's proof that success is not about where you start in life, but about where you strive to go.

So are the other 14 contributors in this book.

Know that you *can* find that elusive (or maybe not-so-elusive) "something" for which you're searching and create the change you desire.

You *can* have it all!

Turn the page to discover powerful stories and insightful advice from people who have discovered the same—so you can write your own story of success.

# Chapter 1

## Finding Your GRIT

By Dr. Dene Eller

Growing up, I wished every day was Sunday. That was the day Dad gave us a break from the physical violence, domestic abuse, and heavy drinking that filled the rest of our week. Sunday, he took a rest, because it was "God's time."

It's funny then, that one of my most painful childhood memories is also the dreading of one particular Sunday. Earlier on that week, it had been blazing hot—the type of summer days when only a juicy, sweet watermelon could really hit the spot. That's what led me, and my childhood gang of three, to steal watermelons from the preacher's garden. In our childish arrogance, we thought we'd gotten away with our crime. Alas, the preacher had seen everything from his kitchen window.

Less than a thousand people lived in my sleepy textile town in the rural South. Each and every one of them had gotten the news of my misdeed by sundown. That's also about the time I got home and was greeted by my Granny on the porch. Switch in hand, she was ready to punish me with what she called "a life experience." My behind still ached come Sunday morning. Plus, I was filled with dread, knowing soon, I'd see the preacher and find out God's judgment of me to add to my physical pain.

As we left church, the preacher greeted me with a slight grin and a hint of a chuckle in his voice. He stared into my eyes and said, "God has already forgiven you; the gates of heaven are still open." The deep frown in Granny's brow since the incident came to light melted away to nothing. I had not been cast out.

I continued to attend church every Sunday morning without fail. Sitting with my family in the first pews, I was being indoctrinated into deep southern Baptist beliefs and moral principles.

The start of each new week held the fragile hope that the peace of Sunday would carry over. It never did. I began to blame myself for how things were. My time spent in the pews had taught me that people were punished for misdeeds, so I figured I must be getting punished for something I had done wrong. If I were a better person, I thought, then there would be no more violence. Daddy's temper would subside, and life in our 800-square-foot cinder-box duplex would be perfect, right? I began examining my faults constantly, my brain playing a non-stop tape of my voice reiterating "I-AM-A-FAILURE." I kept working to be the best version of myself I could be. I did as I was told, and followed the good book, yet things remained as they had always been.

Eventually, things did change ... when my parents divorced. That was not the end result I had hoped to achieve with my efforts. I took it as proof that the voice in my head was right; I was a failure and always would be. I believed I was doomed to repeat my mother's perilous life. It was my destiny to never escape our single-stoplight, dull town and follow her path. I could see the life that lay ahead of me clearly: barely making ends meet, working as a "lint head" (the nickname workers in the cotton mill were given) next to the same people I'd known since I was born. Then, I'd start my own family, and my children would follow me into the mill, too.

At school, I enjoyed the company of my friends so much that I was labeled "an academic underachiever." PE was the one place I shone. I was a runner, and both my junior high and high school PE coaches saw something within me no one else had ever noticed: fire. They had the ability to draw out my potential and fan the flames when I couldn't see past the horizon of my troubles. They inspired me to strive for my personal best and encouraged me by showing enthusiasm for my talents, as well as genuine caring and unconditional love for me as a student. The first shifts in my mindset were a direct result of the relationships I had with these important people in my life.

Still, escaping town to attend college seemed an impossible dream … until the meeting between me, my mother, a few of my mother's friends from church, and the preacher. They were wondering how they could best help our family. When I was asked what would be beneficial for me, I uttered my secret desire—I wanted to go to college. The church committee did not agree with my perception of it being out of reach. They called the local Baptist college, which the preacher had ties to, and I was accepted as a student. Taking that single risk in uttering those words gave me all I ever wanted—escape.

The college was within driving distance of where I'd grown up, but it may as well have been a different country for how dissimilar it was to all I'd ever known. For the first time in my life, I experienced the opposite of surviving—thriving. I had very little in terms of material things … no car or nice clothes. But I cherished my new sense of freedom as if it were a precious gem.

I dedicated myself to my studies in a way I had never been able to before. Without having to negotiate family drama on a daily basis, I was able to stay focused, learn and apply new concepts, and complete tasks with ease. My newfound joy of learning led me to take my first steps off my mother's path and onto my own. College confirmed the mill would never be for me, but becoming an educator would. After three years of studying, I graduated not only with honors, but debt-free, too.

The fire within me, which had gotten me out of my small town, then empowered me with the courage to go where women had not gone before—I became the first woman patrolman in Chapel Hill, NC, and the first woman vetted for detective by my police force. Being the first to take on these roles was thrilling, and I received recognition—something I had never gotten while growing up. It also allowed me to realize the courage, resolve, and grit I had within me, and what I could achieve when I put them to use.

While trailblazing within my law enforcement agency was something I was immensely proud of, after three years, I grew to loathe the stressful environment. My instincts told me that police work was not what I was supposed to be doing. I returned to education, working as a teacher for a few years before being offered a graduate teaching fellowship across the country in Oregon. This was an incredible opportunity I instinctively wanted to take. However, the fear of leaving the stable home and career I'd worked so hard to attain compelled me to reject the offer—a response I regretted more and more as the weeks of summer passed by.

I stayed in touch with the professor who had offered me the position and, possibly sensing my regret, she asked me again to become a part of her team. This was it! I knew I had to risk all I had built and grab onto the opportunity. My mom, whose life still revolved around the small town I came from, said it was a mistake. I understood her fears, but I knew what I had to do. I packed all my belongings into a pickup truck and drove across the United States to my new life.

Shortly after beginning my first term in my new position, Mom's warning rang in my ears when all the graduates in my department were told our college was being downsized and eliminated in one year. I was devastated. My professor told me not to worry, because she had accepted a position in New Hampshire, and I could work with her there. Having just packed up my life from one side of the country to come to Oregon, she was now asking me to do it all again to move back to the East

Coast. Just as I had instinctively known taking the chance to be in Oregon was what I had to do, I immediately sensed that I would not be moving back across the country. For the first time in my life, I had the courage to let go and allow what *could* happen to begin to happen.

I realize now that this very moment in which I decided to stay in a strange new place and "let go" was the culmination of all of my experiences up to that point ... and of my "never-give-up" mindset. It was as if I'd left behind my childhood baggage, once and for all, when I packed up the pickup.

Now, my mindset was set on success.

With the limitations of my childhood no longer impeding me, I was able to step up with courage, harness my grit, and do whatever I set out to achieve.

I went on to continue my graduate studies and was awarded a Distinguished Graduate Student honor for my service to the university. I received the same award for service during my doctorate, where I accelerated and completed my PHD in three years instead of the typical five to seven. I was the first woman in my family to earn three college degrees and a PhD.

I couldn't have done it alone—no one can. My path crossed with that of many outstanding people who cared about my well-being along the way: the sport coaches who saw the fire in me, the pastor who helped me get into college, and the professor who asked me to move across the country.

Now, I've made it my life's work to do my best to pass forward the gifts my champions gave me.

When it comes to harnessing the power of your mind, my best advice is to *adapt quickly to a letdown*. Take the time to process any grief in your life. Reflect, feel your feelings, and as fast as you can, let your disappointment heal and take healthy steps forward. How?

First, *acknowledge what happened* by assigning meaning to the event that caused the hardship.

Second, *dig for the positives*, and write them down. In doing so, you begin to build an optimistic perspective, which in turn strengthens your new positive mindset.

Third, and most importantly, learn to *manage your disappointment* with a written inventory of what was in or out of your control.

Taking action on these three deliberate steps will build your grit, inner strength, resiliency, and self-confidence.

**You CAN Have It All!** I am proof that success is not about how you started in life, but where you strive to go. I have achieved all that I have by harnessing the power of my thoughts, utilizing the resilience I built through my childhood, learning from the insights I gained along the way, and listening to my instincts that *always* know the right thing to do. My living legacy is to light that ember of self-belief and fan those flames in as many people as possible.


Dr. Dene Eller (a.k.a. Dr. SUCCESS coach) has spent her professional life empowering others to reach peak performance. Throughout her educational and coaching career, she has successfully reinvented herself multiple times. She has vast experience as a winning sports coach on every level and has served on college and university faculties. She's career counseled on the high school and college level, and is a licensed public school administrator. As a seasoned K-12 educator, she has been heralded amongst her peers as an A.C.E. (A Champion in Education) recipient for outstanding teaching and service for the last five consecutive years. Dr. Eller has earned leadership ranks and served as an executive team leader in several direct sales companies. Her expertise and professional training as a Life Coach have been chiefly responsible for hundreds of clients breaking monthly sales track records. You can learn more about her here: https://www.facebook.com/AskSmartMoneyCoach.

**Get Dr. Eller's gift to you, her "How to Become a Fierce Smart Money Hero" for real-life lessons from a teacher and money coach, here: https://hopebookseries.com/gifts/.**

# Chapter 2
## Losing It All to Find Myself

*By Dr. Emily L. Cross*

Some people hate clichés. I happen to be one of them.

But, in my case, the event that "changed it all" occurred on what really *was* a dark and stormy night.

It was February, a few days after the world celebrated love with red roses and delicious chocolates on Valentine's Day. The rain pelted down on my windshield as I maneuvered through the oddly empty streets to my little suburban home after an empty day at work.

I arrived to an eerily black house. It looked empty.

But his car was parked out front.

It shouldn't have been. He was supposed to be working. He should have been at least pretending he worked.

Plus, I was craving silence. I wanted an evening alone, wrapped up on the couch in an oversized blanket, drinking a hot mug of tea and watching reality TV.

I walked in tentatively. The house was deserted. His car was there. But he wasn't.

It didn't feel right.

My phone buzzed. An influx of text messages started: "You never loved me," "You only used me for my money," and the grand finale, "You ruined my life."

I knew he was drinking. And not the casual, happy hour beer, either. It was the "I never made it to work and have been drinking all day" type of beer. It was the "drinking until I am angry" beer. In fact, I'm sure it wasn't even beer; he'd likely been drinking a lot of something stronger.

If you're not familiar with alcoholism, or have never been trapped in the dysfunction of an abusive relationship before, you may be fortunate enough to *not* know what it's like walk on eggshells around your partner, or to blend into the silent shadows of the hallway so he won't notice you. You hold your breath … bite your tongue … look away. You exist silently. Invisibly. Because existing with breath—breathing life into your voice—ends in destruction: of pictures, dishes, self-worth, value, identity, and more.

I knew the night wasn't going to end well.

And it didn't.

The next few hours were a blur of yelling. Crying. Hurting. Hoping someone would help.

It ended with me hiding in a pile of stuffed animals. From a man I once loved, wielding an AR-15.

The buzz of my phone interrupted the silence around me.

"When are you coming?" and "Are you OK?" "You were supposed to pick up your new shirts hours ago."

"Is your husband home tonight? I might need some help," I typed into my phone.

The quiet outside indicated that I might possibly be able to get out of the house. So, I quietly crept out, but the overwhelming urge to run hit me hard. So, I did.

I tried to stop breathing. I tried to become the invisible voice I had spent years refining. I needed to disappear. I was being hunted.

Not 20 minutes later, help arrived. It wasn't my friend's husband, but the local police, "Emily? It's safe. You can come out. We have him in the back of the car. It's okay."

And although the rain was still pouring in heaps outside my house, I immediately felt a shift.

I had survived. But, I was also done just "surviving."

The moral of the story is this:

*Your voice is your superpower.*

You can use it to protect yourself. You can use it to protect others.

The shift that occurred within me that night was in *recognition* of the irony of my life.

You see, my life's work has consisted of teaching others how to harness the power of their words to help them improve their relationships, overcome fear, affect change, and/or get in front of an audience.

A little ironic, right? From the one whose truth was silence?

Words have always been my space. I preach that they are your foundation—the way you create the world you want. And when you truly become an empowered communicator, you can conquer any mountain.

I learned it. I taught it and saw the lives of my students changing. I believed wholeheartedly in the truth of my teachings.

But I didn't think that I deserved that same gift of freedom my students were experiencing.

After years living in dysfunction, I silenced myself. I believed that although others may deserve to take up space with their insight, ideas, and knowledge—my only space for doing so was in a classroom.

I watched my life unravel. Not once. Not twice. But many times over. At some point, I decided to use my voice to protect people, and their images, *instead of protecting myself.* I watched myself fade into darkness as I hid from the words that would keep me safe. I hid behind the words people expected from me.

I know the night of this story should never have happened. But I was fearful of using words that would have kept me safe. I was afraid. Afraid of using words that would ruin his shining reputation. Afraid of saying anything at all, because I didn't want his Christian community to look at him in any other way than adoration. I didn't want his family to know. Or mine.

I was the shining star. The Ph.D. The strong woman. The mom. The healer. The smiles. The laughter.

*I was joy.*

And people who are joy don't live in unsafe spaces.

People who are strong don't tolerate the abuse that is inherent in alcoholism.

And moms don't allow their children to live in dysfunction.

I didn't say anything, because of fear. Fear of judgment. Fear of failure. Fear of more loss than I could imagine. Fear that I would have to rebuild a life that had already been taken and shaken.

Chaos had been my "safe" space.

And silence had become my truth.

I thought hiding behind a facade of narratives the world expected to hear would keep me, and my kids, safe from the chaos that festered inside our home. I learned to hide behind words I knew people would accept.

I was sure that weaving a story of love, patriotism, intelligence, and a perfectly blended family who lived behind the walls of the tiny little house in the storybook Californian town would protect us.

And it did.

Until it didn't.

That man *chose* not to kill me that night. I know if he wanted me dead, I would be.

That was the impetus for *finally* recognizing that I, just like every student I had spent years gifting the power of voice, also deserved to take up space with my words, ideas, thoughts, and needs. I finally learned that by protecting other people, I was indeed putting myself, my family, and our future in jeopardy.

I learned silence is often life or death. In my case, finally trusting myself to use the right words saved my life.

Since that dark and stormy night, the shift I mentioned is still my guide. Because when you trust yourself and your voice, using your voice and your words to create the dynamics that will elevate you, *anyone* can have it all.

I also realized that "having it all" sometimes means going back to having nothing. I had to leave behind everything I held dear to set myself free from the prison of the narratives that were guiding my life. I had to break the untruths I had been telling myself, and the world, to get help from the person I had been protecting.

I had to lose it all to find myself.

Holding on to the narratives that people assigned to me—and those that others entrusted me to propagate—was the path to my demise. Emotionally, mentally, and ultimately, physically. I learned that to create to the world I wanted to thrive in, I had to adopt *my own* narratives to define who I was, my capabilities, and my responsibilities to myself and my community.

The truth is, it isn't always easy. It requires work, and there are always ways you can improve. Often, the finish line seems to move *just* when you think you have reached your pinnacle.

The key is to first *decide* that you are worth it, and then, commit to that decision. You must be willing to invest the time and the work into yourself. Next, you actually have to DO THE WORK! Mindset and personal development work go together, or frankly, they don't really work at all.

Where has this work gotten me? First, it saved my life. It saved the lives of my kids. It also brought me back to life emotionally and spiritually. No longer do I hide from myself to protect others.

Professionally, I created a space where my voice not only supports me, but other business owners, too, so they can thrive in a competitive small-business market. I founded not one, but two companies to help people raise their game in business: The Wordwell Mag, a digital publication to elevate branding for local businesses, nonprofits, and community members, and The Wordwell Group, a coaching and consultancy for speakers and writers. The common goal? To empower leaders, coaches, and entrepreneurs with the gift of words.

This professional growth not only supports me financially, but has provided me with the freedom to spend more time with my family, support my community, and most importantly, to take up space in a world I know I belong in.

Now, I truly do have it all! I wake up every day asking, "What next?" because I know the only limits I have to face are those I burden myself with.

If you can relate to the loss of voice I went through, I'd love to offer you the following advice:

Truth flows in words. The best step you can take in discovering your voice and purpose is by writing. Some people would call such pages a "journal" or "diary." I call them my "Wake-Up Call." Life makes more sense when we write it out. Ideas become more logical (or illogical, in some cases), truths become hard to ignore, and goals become more concrete.

Dedicate the first 30 minutes every day to writing. There is no "right" or "wrong" way—all you have to do is write. Allow the words to flow from your pen to paper. You might feel like you're rambling, but somewhere in the middle of it, you will find yourself.

At first, it may be in bits and pieces. Sometimes, the truth will flow faster than your fingers can write.

After three months, dedicate an afternoon to reading your pages. What themes come up? What goals do you have? What is the one frustration that repeatedly pops up?

Soon, you'll have your own wakeup call. You'll begin to see who you are, what you represent, and where you want to go. *You will find your truth.* You will begin the process of finding your voice, your power, and your value on paper. It's tangible. It's real. It's you.

And don't worry; your dark and stormy night will be followed by a lull. In that lull, learn how to trust yourself, humbly, by listening. Dig deep and do the hard work of finding yourself and your voice. Then, use it … because **You CAN Have It All!**


Emily Cross, Ph.D. is an inspiring speaker, published author, and celebrated voice. After a noted career in higher education, Dr. Cross transitioned to share the power of words with the small business, entrepreneurial, and non-profit community. Dr. Cross is committed to ethical, honest, and authentic communication. Dr. Cross knows good communication practices lead to higher sales, success, and happiness. You can learn more about her here: https://www.wordwellgroup.com.

**Get Dr. Cross' free gift, a strategy session to help you discover how to ignite your business through creative communication strategies to engage, excite, and educate your audience, here—you'll walk away with a game plan to confidently show up to your audience: https://hope-bookseries.com/gifts/.**

# Chapter 3

## In the Shadow of the Rainbow

### By Cathy Domoney

I used to have a disturbing recurring dream.

I was about to move out of a house, and while showing the new owners around before leaving, I discovered a whole heap of amazing rooms I had not even realized existed. Every time I had the dream, I felt disappointed that I had never had a chance to enjoy those beautiful rooms, and now, it was too late.

Back in the early days when I was a new mum to (only) two young kids, I felt as though I were in a deep, dark hole. I could glimpse the colorful, wonderful world outside, but I didn't have the inclination, energy, or motivation to climb out.

My beloved late dad once asked me how I could be depressed when I had everything to be happy about and grateful for. My husband—my childhood sweetheart—echoed the question. And I knew I had a beautiful life … one to be envied! Didn't I love being a mum? Yes! Didn't I like being there for my kids? Absolutely! I have always been immensely proud of the people we are raising. So why was I so down, when we had worked so hard to create the exact life we wanted? I could not answer my husband, as I was as confused as he was.

Therein lies the rub: I knew on an intellectual level how lucky and blessed I was in all areas of my life, but my emotions did not match my thoughts. I felt an unexplained emptiness—a lethargy—and I lived an unenthusiastic existence.

The irony was that I also had the training to know what I could/should do to get myself out of it, but I could not (at that time) find the will to implement any of the options available to me.

I came to understand that all my unhappiness was related to my body weight and shape. I kept myself prisoner as self-punishment, and self-blame became my routine. At one point, I did not leave the house for several weeks, hiding myself away from the outside world.

But then, I had a life-changing experience.

I watched a documentary film called *Embrace*. It hit my soul so hard that I quietly wept in the cinema while it played. One of the biggest smack-in-the-face-with-a-shovel moments was when I saw women who were far curvier than me learning to embrace who they are. I could see their beauty and their magnificence, but not my own.

It did not make any sense to me whatsoever, which finally motivated me to dig deep to find out what the heck was going on within me. What I discovered would change the direction of my life forever.

I realized that the reason I could not embrace who I was had nothing to do with my dress size, but rather the fact that I was not living the full life I had always dreamt of. I was in desperate need to manifest something else—the other half of my life that had been missing—my professional life.

But how? And when? My family was growing in size, and I found myself repeating the following lies about following my dreams:

*"I'll wait until I have more time."*

*"I'll do it when I have lost all the extra weight."*

*"I'll do it when the kids are grown."*

*"I'll do it when I have more energy."*

*"I'll do it once my husband gets another promotion."*

*"I'll do it when life calms down a little."*

*"I'll do it when my autoimmune stuff settles."*

These exact thoughts (excuses) kept me stuck for over a decade. It was only with the birth of my last child that I realized there was no more time to waste and no more places to hide.

Beginning her journey to join us prematurely (and in a whirlwind of drama at 2:00 a.m. while her daddy was interstate), I nearly died giving birth to my youngest. Then followed a gruellingly beautiful six months at home with my perfect, new, doll-sized daughter and four older children. The pressure was on (and on me alone): if she did not feed well and put on weight, she would have to go back into hospital, which was an hour away from me. My husband was still interstate; my other four children still needed me as much as always; I had no family around to support me; and I was in immense physical pain from my traumatic surgeries (a dangerous c-section and painful sterilization). To make matters even worse, I contracted the flu and lost two important friendships during this time.

It was quite literally the best and worst time of my life. I honestly do not know how I got through it, but it taught me some essential lessons.

The lost friendships taught me that I do not need anyone. Don't get me wrong; I LOVE people, I LOVE connections, and I LOVE my friendships; however, I now know that I will survive if they are taken away from me, despite the pain and heartache. I realized that I had been scared: of making changes, of becoming successful, and of losing friends.

Guess what? Keeping quiet and my ambitions under wraps did not save my friendships anyhow. They could tell I was not being 100% authentic, and they left. So why not embrace the fullness of the life I truly desired? I learned to take comfort in the knowing that the right people would stay, and the right people would go. Plus, here's a little secret: when the wrong ones leave, they make room for new and wonderful people to come into your world!

The physical pain of two surgeries taught me that I was stronger than I could ever have possibly imagined, and that despite the personal physical and emotional struggle I faced, I was still a dedicated mum doing her very best. When I received the kids' school reports and awards they had won that year and saw how brilliantly they had done, I felt so proud and relieved that I cried. I was so grateful to have managed to still be there for them 100% through it all. I knew then that I could face any challenge my potential business could throw at me and still rock it as a mama!

Finally, the physical and emotional pain I endured, along with the strange grief I experienced when I nearly died during delivery, taught me that time is truly precious. I had no more to waste, because tomorrow is not promised.

Six months after my littlest was born, my first client literally banged down my door. I proceeded to then spend an hour and a half trying to convince her that I was the wrong person to help her! True story!

She was a local mother who had resonated with my philosophies that I had shared with her during our discussions on raising/teaching children and wanted me to coach her teen son. He had become depressed, was having disruptive outbursts, and had pretty much given up on life. Driven to help, I worked with him for a few weeks, and this amazing young man turned his life around! His confidence soared, and he started succeeding in all areas of his life. Helping him helped me, too—that spark to follow my dream was reignited after having been extinguished for far too long.

*"Okay universe,"* I thought. *"I hear you, and so I shall begin."*

I had an abundance of expertise and experience already; I have always been amazing at manifesting, and very intuitive. It was time to unleash it all!

I embarked on a journey of self-discovery. I learned to unplug from the outside world and to be very protective of my energy. I got quiet and went inward.

Some made fun of all the new things I was trying, courses I was taking, and gurus I was seeking out, but it did not bother me. Finally, I felt energized, alive, and aligned. Every "no" brought me closer to a "yes." Every explored possibility brought me closer to my direction, and every person who faded away (because he or she did not agree with or understand my journey) brought me to the most amazing connections and blessings of opportunities.

What followed was nothing short of miraculous! I began manifesting my business like a queen! And opportunities just fell in my lap:

I officially started my business, Miracle-Ready Mindset, at age 40.

I published my children's picture book series.

I invested in myself and began working with the most excellent mentors in the industry.

I launched my online courses.

I worked with the most incredible thought leaders on the planet.

I started getting invited to join in global events with my heroes in the industry and travel globally.

I was (am) interviewed frequently.

I have been featured in major media outlets such as TED. com, The Today Show, and Buzzfeed.

As my life evolved, I learned an alternative to the shadowed struggle; I began to embrace and dance with the depression that had previously kept me stuck. I realized that it does not define me, but is rather a beautiful part of who I am.

Why beautiful?

Because it has taught me so much about my soul and spirit! It taught me that I was living only half a life.

Now, I have manifested my dream life!

Can you relate to my story?

If you have a nagging feeling that you too can BE more—everything you were born to be—NOW is the best time to do it!

The first step? Decide on your "all." What does it look like for you?

Then, get out there and grab it!

Here is my best advice for getting started:

Show-up for yourself.

Choose yourself.

Believe in yourself.

Invest in yourself.

Specifically, following are four actions steps to beginning your journey:

**1. Do the Toxic Work:** Write down all the negative thoughts you have in all areas of your life. Keep writing until you feel you are done. (Yes, this can take a while!)

**2. Do the Light Work:** Start thinking about what kind of thoughts you need to start thinking to fill the void and bring you closer to your goals. (This is mindset work, and it makes ALL the difference!)

**3. Be Resistance Ready:** Get ready for it, because it's sure to come! Not only from yourself, either, but also from people around you. Change (even good change) can be scary, but fear

---

is a part of growth … so get comfortable with it and move through it.

**4. Design Your Life:** Begin to actively design your life. Get very detailed about what will happen, when, how you will FEEL when it does, and write it all down. Let your imagination go wild!

**Perhaps most importantly, never give up, even when things feel impossible!**

It was only two years ago that I decided to create my dream life, so I could really have it all. I achieved success from my living room, building an incredible business while juggling three auto-immune diseases and raising five kids (three of whom have the beautiful gift of Autism).

And I don't have the house dream anymore; I am now using all my rooms!

**You CAN Have It All**, too! Choose the exact life you want, and make it happen. If not now, when? If not us, who? Go chase your dreams! You can be part of a wave of women badasses who are "businessing" our way, on our terms, for the new world we are creating for the next generation.

Transformational leader Cathy Domoney is a mother of five, inspirational author, teacher, and professional mentor who uses mindset hacks and the Law of Attraction to propel her clients to next-level success, fast! You can learn more about her here: https://www.cathydomoney.com.

**Get Cathy's gift, a 20-minute Breakthrough Call with her to begin forming your strategy for next-level success here: https://hopebookseries.com/gifts/.**

# Chapter 4

## Through Struggle, We Reach the Stars

By Samantha Touchais

For most of my career in international marketing, I have been very fortunate to have worked for some of the world's largest consumer companies. I was well-respected in my field and had a high-flying career. But the hours were long, and the expectations high. Competition was fierce, and jealousy was rife throughout the marketing team.

I love working with people, bouncing ideas off each other and supporting one another through the hard times. But while working for a world-famous company, I ended up with an absolute tyrant for a boss.

And the situation was sucking the life out of me.

Plus, as a young mum, it was impossible to juggle the demands of my job with those of a young child. To add to the struggle, from 2015 on, my family and I were hit with one hard time after another. Sudden unemployment meant facing losing the rental home we adored. Our beloved identical twin boys, Maxime and Théodore, died at birth, and I was diagnosed with a life-threatening chronic illness that scared the living daylights out of me. Our youngest son was born prematurely and nearly died during birth.

Through all of this, I was living on the other side of the world from my parents. My mother had recently had her third stroke and was set to undergo heart surgery.

Life was hard, but it is through struggles that we reach the stars, and I decided that I was going to take hold of the reins and steer my life in a better direction.

It was after going through these hardships and tragedies that I decided life as I knew it was not what I had signed up for. I wasn't finding the true happiness and balance that I craved and needed.

I fought hard with the belief that focusing on my needs was selfish, but then that old, famous airline adage about putting your own oxygen mask on before helping others came to mind. I could feel myself running on empty, and the patience and compassion I needed to be the best wife, mother, daughter, and friend certainly wouldn't come from an empty tank.

It was during this difficult time that I became very clear on what I was on earth to do. No, there wasn't any mystical moment when a light shone down on me from Heaven. It was more of a slow drip feed of feelings that gently and lovingly opened my eyes to the path I was supposed to follow—that of leading people on a journey of self-discovery to live their best life. I could see so many people around me living on autopilot, and I wanted to show them how to live consciously and with purpose, while creating a mindset for success.

Because the truth is, *mindset matters above everything.*

I started reading every book I could get my hands on about the brain, our belief system, and the ego. I studied mindfulness and life coaching and received my certification in both. I then completed a master's certification in Neuro Linguistic Programming.

The years of study paid off, as I am now working as a business and mindset coach. I work with clients to not only uncover hidden beliefs, but to remove the ones that don't serve them ... thereby creating a mindset for success and abundance.

And I love it! I enjoy a wonderful balance between family life and work life, and I get to be with my children as they grow up (something I never got to do working long hours in the corporate world and traveling the globe for my previous job). I have also written and published three books and have several more on the way.

Plus, something truly miraculous came out of my new mindset and visualization abilities. I have recovered from my life-threatening illness—something my extremely well-qualified and respected medical specialist is calling a "miracle"—a word he said he has never used before.

Am I living my dream life? Absolutely! Did I create this for myself by getting clear on my vision and trusting my instincts to guide me? You bet! I feel very blessed to have come out on the other side of tragedy having found myself in such a wonderful position to be able to help others. It is my passion and my calling, and all is as it should be.

The truth is, life perpetually throws challenges at us. Sometimes, it even seems as if there is a bias toward some of us more than others. But you can master your mindset and change any situation you are in ... because every situation starts with the mind.

It is only in recent years that scientists discovered that our brains are malleable right up to the day we die. In other words, you *can* actually teach an old dog new tricks! It also means that no one is "too old"—or "too anything"—to live the life of his or her dreams.

Yes, even you!

So, what can you do to create the life you truly want and deserve? It all starts in the mind. Before any manifestation and creation can take place, it is crucial to ensure you have the right mindset for success. No matter how good you are at visualizing an outcome or writing down your goals, if your mindset is not set for success, you simply will not achieve your goals. There is no exception to this.

My coaching is based on what I call my A+ Process—a powerful four-step process that teaches you to:

- AWAKEN to your purpose,
- ALIGN with your why,
- ACT on your learnings, and …
- ACHIEVE your dreams and goals.

In other words, it helps you get really clear on what you want in your life, and to create and then take the steps needed to get there.

If you're ready to get started on that path, complete the following exercise. You'll need some paper and a pen. (Call me old-fashioned, but I believe the best way to map out your dream life starts with a piece of paper and your favorite pen. The combined action of thought and the physical act of writing cements in your brain what it is you want.)

**Exercise: Create Your Dream Life**

**Step 1.**

*AWAKEN - Get crystal clear on what you want.*

What does your dream life look like? Who is in your dream life? Where are you living? What do you do every day? Are you surrounded by friends, family, children, famous people? How much money are you earning and how? What do you do for fun? Get really clear on all the elements of the life you want to live.

*Write it down.*

**Step 2.**

*ALIGN - Visualize your dream life, and start to feel it.*

What feelings come up for you when you imagine this life? Does it feel possible? Or do you feel resistance? If resistance is coming up for you (and you will know if it is by how you physically react to your vision; often, a heavy feeling in the stomach or a weight on the shoulders occurs), then you need to work on your mindset and beliefs.

**Step 3.**

*ACT – Determine the steps needed to achieve your goal.*

Now it's time to map out what needs to happen to achieve your goal. There is a false belief that manifesting your dream life means that you visualize what you want, ask for it, and then release that request. Like magic, it will come to you. This is where most people go wrong.

We are expected to take action ourselves. The Universe will guide us and provide help, but we are co-creators *with* the Universe, not just receivers.

A great first step is to answer these questions:

- What can I do in the next week to get started toward my goal?
- What can I do in the next month?
- In the next year?

The trick here is to take action—any action. Even if it feels like the tiniest, most insignificant thing, it is already something. Momentum can only start to build when you take that first step, and once you do, you will find that it starts to get easier and easier.

**Step 4.**

*ACHIEVE – Now you are ready to step into your dream life!*

The creation of a dream life doesn't always happen immediately. It all depends on how far away you are from your goal, your mindset, and how much you *really* desire what it is you are asking for.

While you work on each of these steps, be sure to stay in a state of gratitude—an important part in manifesting. By gratitude, I mean giving thanks for the things you already have. A gratitude diary is a great tool to practice gratitude. I suggest buying yourself a notebook, and begin by writing down five things you are grateful for every day. Really take your time to feel the gratitude as you write. Soon, you will find yourself noting things you had not even been aware of before, and you will start to realize how abundant you already are.

The Universe is like a mirror; you get back what you put out. So, watch your thoughts and your feelings, and try to keep them as positive as you can. We all have stressful or negative moments, and that is okay. Try to ensure that at least 51% of your day is spent creating positive energy and sending out positive thoughts, and you will be well and truly on your way to your dream life.

I am often asked how I am so strong. How did I get through all of those devastating challenges without collapsing and staying down?

The answer is my faith, my boys, and my mindset. That is what perpetually gets me back up and moving forward.

I am truly grateful for all the challenges and struggles I have faced. While I never, I repeat NEVER, want to go through them again (or anything similar), I realize what a gift they have been. Even though our beautiful baby boys are no longer here on earth with us, as hard as that still is and always will be, they are still my sons, and I am still their mother … and they are waiting for us to join them one day in Heaven.

I learned through my studies that we carry the DNA of our children in our blood, so I can still carry them with me, literally and figuratively, in my heart.

I truly believe that **You CAN Have It All!** It's all about your mindset—how you choose to view the circumstances in your life. I hope completing the exercise above puts you on your path to true abundance and joy.

Samantha Touchais is a business and mindset coach, specializing in launching dream businesses, mindfulness, mindset coaching, and the creation of good mental habits. With the right mindset, anything is possible, and Samantha has enjoyed helping thousands of people on their journey to designing the right life for them by taking conscious action in everything they do. The creator of The Well-Being Series, author, and coach, she has a keen ability to understand her audience and the issues they are facing. With a talent for putting into words the message an audience needs to hear, she is also a featured meditation teacher on one of the world's largest meditation apps, Insight Timer. Samantha has written and published three books; two for children (*Cai Learns to be Brave* and *The River of Dreams*) and recently her first adult novel, *A Lifetime of Goodbyes*. You can learn more about her here: https://www.samanthatouchais.com.

**Get Samantha's free gift, a complimentary 30-minute strategy call, to discover how to begin turning your passion or dream into a profitable business and/or how your mindset is holding you back from achieving the success you desire by scheduling it here: https://hopebookseries.com/gifts/.**

# Chapter 5

## The Key to Traversing Difficult Times

*By Vanessa Zamora*

Over the years I spent trying to establish myself as an independent insurance agent, I felt the same way Tom Edison must have as he struggled to invent the lightbulb. After one of his many unsuccessful attempts, he said: "I didn't fail. I have just found ten thousand ways it *didn't* work."

I never thought I would end up selling insurance, as I had always been an employee in a whole different line of work. Doing something outside of that "box" made me feel uncertain and uneasy, because I didn't know if it would work for me. I wasn't sure I could become successful doing it alone. I didn't see a structured way of doing business, as I was used to being told what my duties are at my place of employment and everything already being set in stone when it came to performing my daily job.

Yet I've been accustomed to the world of life insurance most of my life, because my parents used to sell it. They both worked as managers for a big company in Manila, Philippines called Coco Life Insurance. I would watch them get ready for work and leave looking very professional.

I remember being about ten or eleven years old and hearing them talk about their business deals. They would be so excited when they struck a deal with a huge account for a big company. That was a pivotal time, and the excitement just reverberated in the house.

At the time, I didn't understand what life insurance was. So, my parents explained how it works and why a person should have it. That was my first education about it, and my introduction into the importance of having it in case the income earner of the family dies, so those left behind will have the financial resources needed while they grieve and move on with their life.

I received the next level of education about life insurance when a friend of mine introduced me to the industry.

She was involved in a multi-level networking platform in insurance. She asked me to bring my boyfriend at the time to a meeting with her without telling me what it was all about. When we arrived, she brought us to a conference room in the basement. She had a white binder and proceeded to give us a paper presentation. She and her boyfriend took turns talking about each document in the binder.

We were quite surprised, considering neither had even asked if we were in need of insurance in the first place. I was embarrassed. We had been "pushed" into a presentation. I was also grateful my boyfriend was able to remain polite enough as to not interrupt their presentation, but once it was done, we said our goodbyes and left unimpressed.

Time went on, and I became accustomed to working two if not three jobs to survive financially as a single mom.

I met my fiancé in 2011, just as he was starting medical school. When he graduated, he accepted his residency in Tacoma, Washington. He asked me to go with him, because I was pregnant with our son, and this way, we could raise him together when he was born.

I was depressed about leaving my family, my daughters, and my friends behind, but we took the leap. I knew no one in Tacoma, and the weather affected my depression.

My manager at the time encouraged me to find a job in Tacoma while on maternity leave. I was blessed to be offered one as an On-Call Enroller in the Sales and Marketing Department of the same company I had worked at in California before we moved. At that point, I decided to take a chance and study for the Life Producer Exam, so I could get my license to sell life insurance products just in case I ever decided to apply for Account Manager and sell life insurance on the side.

When I finally took the test, I failed it three times. I was disappointed in myself, but my friend suggested I take the exam in California. The idea was that I might feel more comfortable and confident taking it while I was home visiting family.

So, that's what I did, while a friend watched Andrew in the car parking lot. I was nervous. I doubted myself, thinking I would fail it again. When I finished, my whole body was shaking in anticipation of the results. The woman across from me printed a piece of paper and congratulated me with a smile on her face. I was elated! I ran out of the exam office waving the paper to my friend and screaming, "I've passed!"

Launching myself into the industry, I quickly realized that operating on your own requires so much work! You need to create that "know, like, trust factor" to get clients. You have to build a big network that doesn't include your friends and family, and without one, you have only a slight chance of selling policies. This requires hours and hours of networking, whether that be by attending networking events or cold calling a list of leads if you purchase one.

I felt comfortable giving presentations only to my family and friends, which resulted in only a few policy sales. Aside from those, the only others I 'sold' over two years in the business were my own and my son's. Thankfully, I kept my day job during that time.

I remember thinking to myself, "Maybe I am not capable of doing this. It is not my 'style,' and I am more comfortable being employed. I have daily duties as a single mom, a work schedule to go by, and everything is already cut out for me, so I don't need to figure it all out on my own to be productive. Plus, I have the security of reliable hourly pay."

Selling insurance was not sitting well in my stomach, but I had to keep moving. Being successful with it became my mission, because, at the end of the day, I was driven to educate individuals on how life insurance with Living Benefits can help them financially should a health crisis arise. It's important to me that people are able to recover peacefully and financially sound.

I had been considering buying leads from a broker that would cost me around $250-$1,500. But there was no guarantee of a return on investment. I also hate cold calling people, so the thought of having to do so felt degrading. So, I threw that idea right out of the window. It wasn't me.

Then, I saw a connection's Facebook post about creating a sales landing page, and I reached out to him. He suggested I have one, so people online could immediately find me if they were looking for insurance. This way, I could generate qualified leads who are already in the market for life insurance, which makes for a much easier sell. It sounded too good to be true … until he quoted me the price—$3,000—PLUS a monthly subscription of $97 to Clickfunnels.

I didn't have the funds to invest. Even worse, I went through a series of difficult life events: my dad died in October 2019, the COVID pandemic was on the rise in 2020, and I had multiple accidents that resulted in my termination from another job that was supplementing my income.

By that time, I had spent three years trying to be successful in selling life insurance. I didn't want to give up, but I was feeling hopeless. Then, someone sent me a link to a service similar to Clickfunnels. I signed up for free intending to create my own webpage. As I watched the upgrade video, more opportunities came to mind. I was excited—the investment was less than half of what I had seen before, and I could 'branch out,' too. Not only would I learn how to create my own opt-in page, but I'd offer the same service to other insurance agents and online entrepreneurs who are struggling with online sales as I have!

Talk about a "lightbulb moment"!

I learned how to use the software and offer my newfound skill as a service. I kept my license active, because I love advocating financial literacy and educating others on how to be financially prepared for a health crisis. Because when you lose an income, it's too easy to accumulate medical debt and feel the financial burden. With Living Benefits, though, you are financially secure, and you can recover with a financial peace of mind. I am sure I will continue supporting people in this area in the future.

I have learned so much on this journey. I know what it's like to feel lost during the huge life transitions we all face, whether it be getting divorced, moving to another state, rebuilding your life with a partner, or even losing a family member and experiencing financial turmoil while grieving.

*The key to traversing the difficult times is to dig into the power of the mind.*

In order for me to get to where I am now, I had to overcome the scarcity and competition mindsets. When I did, I created a sort of butterfly effect on the results in my life and business. As I was finding ways to be creative in getting the results I want, I found a new skill, too. And letting go of the expected outcome really created a massive paradigm shift, as did trusting that the process would result in things falling into place instead of thinking they were falling apart.

If you can relate to my story, know that you can clear your mind by pushing out any negative self-talk and the outside noise to get clarity. The first step is in getting quiet. Next, focus on your breathing, taking deep breaths and controlling your inhale and exhale so that the latter is a bit longer than the former. Finally, when your breathing is regulated, concentrate on maintaining the absence of thought. You want to clear each thought that presents itself, so you are thinking of nothing.

This is easier said than done, and it took me years of practice and listening to personal development, manifestation, and affirmation talks and practices. Don't worry—just trust the process and let go of the outcome.

**You CAN Have It All!** No matter where you are in your life right now, you can shift your mindset and change directions. And remember what Edison said about failure. It is not the failure that we should focus on, but how the results can provide another option for becoming a better version of ourselves. In that way, failure is but a steppingstone to our success. It may take you a while to get where you'd like to be, but the climb will be worth it as soon as you see the top.

Vanessa Zamora is now happily married and a full-time stay-at-home mom of three. She is an independent Life Insurance Agent advocating Living Benefits. With three years of experience in the financial services (insurance) field, she is also a Master Funnel Designer. You can learn more about her here: https://www.vanessagorham.com.

**Get Vanessa's gift, a lead magnet page (value 500-$1,000.00) here:** https://hopebookseries.com/gifts/.

# Chapter 6

## Fear Happens in Your Head

*By Lena Thompson*

Do you ever stop and wonder how you arrived at a particular point in your life? Maybe you've felt destined for something *more*, or asked yourself if *this* is really "it."

Having been there before myself, I know exactly what that's like. I wasn't living the life I thought I was meant to. I had no passion or purpose, existing in pure survival mode. I often wondered how the emptiness could feel so heavy. Even worse, I knew I had so much to be grateful for, so why did I feel the way I did?

The feeling of "separation" only intensified after having kids. I wanted so much to be the ideal mom—the one who baked, cuddled up in bed with books, told great stories, and soothed away my children's troubles. But no matter how hard I tried, my anxiety and sense of failure increased. I found myself constantly searching for things around me to fill the void, but nothing helped … at least, nothing that lasted.

Still searching for my identity, I qualified as a Reiki healer and NLP practitioner with the goal of helping others. The problem? I was anxious, stressed, and living in a world of duality as I tried desperately to master my mind while focusing on my demons. This resulted in my pretending to be happy as I struggled to find my own smile.

The turning point came finally came in 2018. Commuting long hours to the office with radio tunes getting on my nerves, I stumbled upon an interview with Dr. Joe Dispenza.

I have been interested in spirituality and passionate about the mind-body connection my entire life. Even as a child, I spent hours wondering where we come from and what happens to us after we die. As a teenager, I read books on these topics. Deep inside, I held on to a "knowing" that we are immortal.

Yet it wasn't until I listened to Dr. Joe describe his own journey of transformation that day—backing up spirituality with scientific data that explained the principle—that I truly began believing what I had always hoped was true: we are so much more than our physical body.

His message—that we have the power to be whoever and feel however we want … that anyone who has a vision for who he or she wants to be in life can be so—shifted and stirred new thoughts and beliefs about myself and my life. For days to come, I listened to his audio books as I drove. I even began looking forward to traffic jams, because they allowed me more time to practice what I was learning—to observe my thoughts and get in touch with my true beliefs and feelings.

I began incorporating daily meditations into my life, which was hard at first. For years, my first instinct was to open my eyes, jump out of bed, and race off to the gym or on a long run. Sitting my body down for meditation required a lot of effort, but I knew it was worth it as I started noticing synchronicities and opportunities coming my way. It was as though the Universe was encouraging me on my journey. Within weeks of incorporating this new routine into my life, I was offered a new contract in London that doubled my then-current pay rate. And, no driving was required!

Through meditation and self-education, I learned that the brain is the record of the past. Doing the same things each day (brushing teeth, the auto-pilot shower routine, taking the same route to work, etc.) becomes our reality.

It's a vicious cycle! We think the same thoughts, which lead to making the same choices we always make. Those choices create the same behaviors that produce the same experiences that ultimately invoke the same emotions, and we're right back to square one: thinking the same thoughts.

The good news, though, is that it *is* possible to change—to interrupt the cycle and create new thoughts and results. In order to do so, *we need to think greater than our environment and circumstances in our lives.*

I was making progress. Although I was a lot happier in my new job, along with the daily meditations successfully taking the edge off of the daily stress and anxiety I experienced, I still had a long journey ahead of me.

In November 2018, I learned that Dr. Joe was coming to the UK to lead a seven-day workshop. I *knew* I had to be there. Seven days away from home and my two children is a long time, but I decided that nothing and no one would stand in my way. I decided to hire an au pair to help for the week, and off I went.

The workshop taught me what meditation is really all about and what I was capable of achieving. Meeting people who cured themselves from terminal or serious health conditions after mainstream medicine gave up on them, and others who, only few days earlier, were in wheelchairs but were now dancing on stage, made me realize how insignificant my problems really were.

I knew one thing for sure: the old aspects of me had to die in order to make room for the person I wanted to become. It all started with changing my thoughts, which was no easy task. It felt like a full-time job to continuously monitor them, stop, actively change them, and start over again.

Determined to shift my mindset, I added daily "Blessing of Energy Center" meditations, focusing on the third energy center, the solar plexus. I visualised it to be made of steel—of unbendable willpower and sense of purpose.

I began to feel stronger, not just physically, but mentally and emotionally. Having spent years trying to please others into liking me, I was finally becoming myself in a world where I felt pressured to be someone else.

For the first time in my life, I felt the energy of passion and purpose. I realized that what happened *to* me in this life is far less significant than my reaction to it. This journey of self-discovery was not only about making external and habit changes, but also about a deep, gradual transformation of my inner perceptions and beliefs.

The problem was that, as I was changing, I was also becoming incompatible with many areas of my life. My old beliefs no longer served me, and it was difficult to find connections and interests to remain tied to my relationships with others. Integrating back into the "real" world was hell—I had changed, while everyone and everything around me remained the same.

Despite being drawn to inspire and heal people, to provide a heart-based service to others, I was still stuck. And despite my progress in mastering my mindset, I still didn't have the confidence to claim my natural gifts.

The self-talk was brutal:

*"Who the hell do I think I am?"*

It was always there, and it always got in the way.

I refused to give up, though, and continued working on my mindset. Finally, a new kind of faith, confidence, and energetic elevation began to slowly emerge. I was learning how to use my newfound power wisely.

The illusions that had been keeping me stuck for so long began dropping away, one after the next, and I slowly started regaining my self-confidence and voice regardless of everything in my life taking a huge hit as I embarked on a journey to entrepreneurship that I knew nothing about. My professional and personal lives spiralled out of control.

Still, I kept moving forward.

In September 2019, I stared my first business, Driving Miss Daisy, to provide companionship and transport services to people who cannot get out and about. I can't tell you how incredible it feels to live with purpose—to help people find their freedom and create new memories!

Equipped with courage and confidence, I quit my six-figure IT job just a few months later.

The thing is, once I realized that the entire material world is nothing but energetic vibration, I understood the importance of keeping energy and vibration levels high. When we vibrate at a certain frequency, we supercharge our ability to heal from almost any physical and emotional pain. We become true masters of our lives and opportunity magnets.

Finally, I found my purpose—to wake myself up, and then, to help others do the same.

And that's how my second business, Nature's Frequencies, was born—I now work with energy-wearable products to help balance and restore the body's natural energy flow to achieve optimal health and wellness.

The more I came to learn about energy and vibration, and the more I saw the incredible results my clients were experiencing, the more content and connected I felt. These were vulnerable people, in physical and emotional pain, who trusted me to help them open their minds to alternative and more holistic ways of healing and living. One spent years in a wheelchair, experiencing daily pain in her knees and back. In just a few minutes, I helped her experience relief. Another was recovering from cancer, and despite having tried pain killers, Reiki, and meditation, it wasn't until I worked with her using our products that all pain left her body. I have so many more stories like these, and each one gave me a strong sense of purpose and meaning in my life.

It often feels surreal that only few months ago, I was on a train to London, doing a job I felt no connection to, and now, I truly feel like I have it all!

The truth is, we live in a culture that is often controlled by fear.

Luckily, we don't need the fear that is designed to protect us, *because we have intuition*—a powerful inner knowing.

There are plenty of studies showing how the intuitive part of our brain knows the "right" answer long before the more analytical part. When you hone your intuitive senses, you make better choices and feel more certain about your actions. You also experience more peace and serenity in your life and pay less attention to things that annoy you or that you disagree with.

To begin developing your intuition, you can:

• **Meditate:** Spending time in silence helps you hear and interpret messages from your intuition.

• **Feel more, think less:** When you no longer believe everything you think, you can clearly see that you are *not* your thoughts.

• **Self-Educate:** Here are some authors I recommend: Neville Goddard, Carolyne Miss, Sonia Choquette, and Dr. Joe Dispenza.

• **Listen:** Your intuition can't speak to you if you're not listening. When you start to take notice, good things will happen, and it will become easier for you to hear.

• **Journal:** Describe your vision of a perfect future. Where would you be? Who would you be with? What would you be doing? Each evening, write down things that went well and things you could improve on next time.

Remember, all our emotions—worry, fear, anger, impatience—they exist *only* in our head. When we are able to get out of our head and follow our intuition, all the external clutter and outside noise goes away. And we become truly free.

**You CAN Have It All!**


Having spent 20 years in IT, Lena Thompson lacked a sense of purpose and fulfilment. Stressed and anxious, she knew her life needed to change, but didn't know where to turn. In 2018, having experienced profound personal transformation, she embarked on a journey of entrepreneurship in the area of health and wellness. Only a few months later, she won the Social Media Marketing award 2019 and was featured in South African Chamber of Commerce and on Essex Business Radio. Her passion and purpose is to help others have an optimal life. You can learn more about her here: https://www.linkedin.com/in/lena-thompson1/.

**Get Lena's gift, a list of resources she used herself on her journey toward entrepreneurship, here:** https://hope-bookseries.com/gifts/.

# Chapter 7

## Tapping into the Power Within

By Michele Duhigg

What if I told you that *you already have everything you need to live a happy, healthy, successful life?* It's true! The most successful people in the world don't have anything you don't have. They just know how to tap into the power within.

I struggled with the same issues for many years. Even though things looked great on the outside, I was full of fear and doubt on the inside.

You see, I did all the things people expected of me. I played sports. I got good grades and even received a full ride academic scholarship to college! After college, I got married and had kids. I was enjoying life—don't get me wrong—but there was a part of me that felt empty inside. Despite my successes, I still battled with self-doubt and never felt good enough. I wasn't truly fulfilled and knew there had to be more to life.

Fast forward 10 years into marriage; I discovered my husband was having an affair, and my whole life collapsed around me. I was in complete disbelief, but what still shocks me to this day was that *I was more worried about how my family would react to the news* than the fact that my marriage was in pieces.

That was a real eye opener!

The following months took me on a journey that allowed me to come into my own and discover who I was and what I wanted out of life. I realized that I had been living my life to please others while failing to be true to myself or what I wanted. But I knew I could change things and live my life on my own terms rather than doing the things that were expected of me. I just had to figure out how.

I became obsessed with personal development and read endless books and articles on the habits of successful people, so I could adopt them as my own. I took self-development courses, worked with coaches, and truly started to recognize the power within myself.

I started practicing mindfulness and meditation, which opened me up spiritually to the belief that we are all connected, energetic beings rather than being constrained by the rules of religion as I always had been before.

Once I discovered the Law of Attraction, the "shoulds" and "shouldn'ts" of religion melted away, and everything clicked for me!

The Law of Attraction (LOA) simply states everything in the Universe is made of energy, which vibrates at different frequencies, and that energy attracts like energy. LOA uses the power of the mind to translate whatever is in our thoughts and materialize it into reality. If we focus on all the negative "doom and gloom," we will remain under that cloud. But if we focus on positive thoughts and have goals that we aim to achieve, we will find a way to achieve them! LOA dictates that whatever can be imagined and held in the mind's eye is achievable!

But it's not as easy as just *trying* to be positive. Most of us have some seriously deep-rooted limiting beliefs that were embedded into our subconscious when we were kids. You see, as children, our Reticular Activating System (RAS)—our brain's filter—categorizes everything we experience into "hurtful or helpful buckets," even before the brain is fully formed and able to recognize anything deeper than what we see right in front of us.

Fast forward to adulthood: more often than not, we are held back by some silly thing that happened when we were seven years old, because we have never taken the time to ditch that belief and replace it with a new one. That means we must intentionally dig up our insecurities and break apart any "truths" we may have previously believed that we no longer want to be held back by (cue my old religious beliefs that fueled more guilt and shame than love and hope!).

But guess what? You can tell your brain exactly what you want to believe! You can choose to fill it with positive, empowering thoughts rather than negative, victimizing ones.

Without limiting beliefs holding you back, the power of LOA can be used to attract and manifest things such as love and relationships, money and wealth, mental and physical health, success, abundance, and so much more!

So how can we start attracting these things into our lives today? Here are a few easy techniques you can start using right away.

### Affirmations

Reciting affirmations is a very effective technique that literally helps us rewire our brains to be more positive. We are affirming ourselves all the time, whether we realize it or not. The problem is that we will believe whatever we tell ourselves regularly. So, if we tell ourselves, *I'm just not smart enough* or *I don't have time*, we will find both to be true.

However, if we repeat carefully crafted, positive statements that focus on what we want to believe, think, and feel (whether we truly feel that way right now or not), *we can change our beliefs to be aligned with our affirmation statements.*

So, rather than feeling unqualified or always stressed for time, we can start replacing those beliefs with more positive ones by using statements such as:

- I believe I can be all I want to be.
- I'm in the process of becoming the best version of myself.
- Stress and limitations are melting away.
- I have the freedom and power to create the life I desire.

Aren't those powerful statements?

**Action Step:** Make a list of affirmations that speak to the areas of your life you struggle with the most and commit to saying them every day for 30 days. Since the brain loves confidence bias, it will look for ways to support your new affirmations, and you will start to form new beliefs in no time!

### Visualization

Another technique to help us maintain a positive mindset and empower our new beliefs is visualization.

Professional athletes and performers all use visualization, because the body does not know the

difference between what is happening and what we imagine is happening. When a runner visualizes a race while attached to electrodes, the exact same sequence of brain activity is observed as when the runner is physically racing.

This is because neurons in our brains interpret imagery the same as a real-life action. In fact, a

study of mental exercises and the impact that it has on strength concluded that by simply visualizing ourselves conducting an exercise, we can increase our strength by 35%.

If visualization can do that, imagine how effective it can be in helping us achieve our goals!

Visualization is a skill I've worked at for a while now. I created vision boards with images of things I wanted to purchase and experiences I wanted to have. I cut out pictures of beautiful homes, new cars, an RV, UTV, a new husband and family, and a job in which I felt fulfilled and made a positive impact on others. And I manifested all of it!

My most recent vision board depicted published authors who help women all around the world. And here I am today, co-authoring the book you're reading right now, because I believed in myself.

I believe you deserve the best out of life, too!

Action Step: Search the web for guided visualizations or for specific help with making your own vision board.

I am so grateful for having discovered this power within myself to truly rewire my brain and enable me to manifest the life of my dreams. It hasn't been easy. Fear and doubt still creep back in every now and then, but I am equipped with the tools to replace those thoughts with ones that align with my new beliefs.

And knowing I am surrounded by my loving husband, family, and friends with the freedom and fulfillment I've always wanted is proof enough that you have the power to completely change your life, too!

**You CAN Have It All!** Everything you need is right inside you. Invest in yourself to learn the skills you need to draw it all out, so you can stop doubting, boost your confidence, and be authentically *you*!

Michele Duhigg is an empowerment coach who helps women look inward to overcome obstacles and live a purpose-led life of fulfillment, freedom, and abundance! You can learn more about her here: https://www.duhiggcoaching.com/.

**Get Michele's free gift, step-by-step exercises to start living your best life now, here: https://hopebookseries. com/gifts/.**

# Chapter 8

## Confessions of a Transformed Corporate Professional

*By Marion Segree*

I have a secret. It's a secret I have kept for many years and have never spoken out loud.

You see, I have been living a double life—the kind few people would be willing to admit to, especially if they had a family.

My secret is I am a closet workaholic! And it was slowly killing me.

This sounds crazy, I know, but I was *addicted* to my job! I couldn't function properly without it. It was as if I had lost my ability to relate to people outside of my work circle. Work became an escape. It was a crutch I used to get out of things I didn't want to do in my personal life. I took my laptop with me everywhere I went. I had virtually no life at all. I was afraid to go out and socialize with friends, because there was this never-ending work I had to complete. I created this monster mentality about work in my head and used it like a shield to protect myself.

What was I trying to protect? Why did I feel so threatened that I couldn't leave my work behind?

I didn't realize it was a problem until the day my world turned upside down.

I remember it clearly. One morning, I was in my kitchen making a smoothie. My daughter was in the hall bathroom with her baby girl, who was standing on the toilet seat, dancing to music while she watched her mother apply makeup.

I listened to my grandbaby's laughter as she enjoyed the music and the time she was spending with her mother and peeked around the corner at them.

My heart froze. My daughter was asleep on her feet, her mascara in hand and raised toward her face! I sprang into action as adrenaline kicked in. I ran toward them and scooped up my grandbaby in one arm and shook my daughter with the other, trying to jolt her awake. I was scared and angry, because I knew something was definitely wrong, and I also knew why. I felt a pain I had never felt grip me in my stomach as I realized she was strung out on some type of drug.

I placed the baby on the couch in the living room and ran into my daughter's room to pack her things. I shoved clothes in a bag and pushed her out the front door, all while rebuking her for bringing illegal stuff into our home. She began to cry, realizing the gig was up; I had finally caught on. She apologized and said she would get help, but I was not listening. I called my parents and my sisters to inform them what happened. One of my sisters sent her daughters to my home to help figure out what to do.

The rest of that day was a blur as numbness took over. We decided as a family to get her into a local detox center as soon as there was a vacant bed and into a rehab immediately after she was discharged. It was going to be a very long 24 hours.

I thought my daughter getting pregnant at sixteen was tough, but no … this was by far the hardest pill to swallow.

I no longer recognized her.

My mind fixated on one word—heroin. I couldn't get past it. I had no idea what a heroin user looked like, let alone what the drug looked like. But I knew my 17-year-old daughter was strung out on it. My body began to shake uncontrollably.

We told my ex-husband and came together as a united family to handle it. I learned more about drugs and drug addiction that day than I ever wanted to. It was enough information to last a lifetime.

That day was also the beginning of a long and rough battle for my daughter's life. Over the course of the next five years, she was in and out of rehabs. I spent thousands of dollars trying to save her. I hoped again and again that it was all a horrible dream I would soon wake up from.

Throughout it all, I was fighting for my corporate job. My boss disrespected and humiliated me several times in front of my peers whenever he felt like it. He tried to intimidate me because I had filed a complaint against him for unfair treatment. Although I contributed fresh, innovative ideas to the organization, they were ignored. I felt as if I was not good enough and would never measure up to their corporate standards.

I did my best to put on a brave front, and I performed my job well all while a silent war waged inside my head and home.

While my daughter battled her own demons and addiction, I battled to keep the job to sustain us all. I was my daughter's champion even when I felt anger and resentment. I held tight to my integrity at work and performed to the best of my abilities.

Over the years, I remained steadfast and continued to add value to the company, but deep inside, I knew it was pointless. Eventually, I lost confidence and was discouraged as I spiraled downward into a negative mindset. I knew I was not where I wanted to be and sought help from my doctor.

She recommended journaling and counseling. I followed her advice and also purchased a set of meditative music online. I listened to this music for 30 days. Doing so achieved two things: it eliminated most of my negative thoughts and retrained my brain. This type of reprogramming is known as brainwave entrainment.

Brainwave entrainment is "a method to stimulate the brain into entering a specific state by using a pulsing sound, light, or electromagnetic field. The pulses elicit the brain's 'frequency following' response, encouraging the brainwaves to align to the frequency of a given beat." (Brainworks Neurotherapy, "Train Your Mind," (https://brainworksneurotherapy.com/types-brainwave-entrainment).

This retraining of my brain helped to put my mind at ease and elevated my thoughts into a positive state. This in turn helped me to function optimally at work. I began to focus on the good things in my job and mentored others on thinking positively.

It was during this time that I thought about starting my own business. I was hesitant, though, because the negative thoughts crept into my psyche and were doing a number on my mind. My phobias resurfaced, and I feared many things, including public speaking and what others thought about me. My inner thoughts crippled me from taking steps to pursue my dream.

I knew my time had run out and my career had come to an end at that company when I was called into my VP's office one morning. Instead of feeling sad, I was elated! I felt as if an enormous weight was lifted off my shoulders. I was finally free!

Free to do what, I didn't yet know. I contemplated my options.

I could use the time to look for another corporate job and "get by" until I was ready to retire. Or, I could take a leap of faith and invest in myself.

I prayed about it and asked God to show me the way. I pondered my options for a couple weeks before I finally made the decision to throw caution to the wind and go for it! I used some of the funds from my severance to settle some bills and the rest to hire a few coaches. I figured I needed to invest in people who were already successful in the digital space and could help shorten my learning curve.

In the beginning, I made a lot of mistakes and learned many valuable lessons along the way. Then, the pandemic hit and threw me a curveball! However, since everyone was forced to work online, it was still the best time to launch my business.

One of my mentors once told me that part of owning a business is hitting rock bottom before finding your feet and rising to greatness. I mean, "rock bottom" for me were dirty words. After all, I saw my daughter hit rock bottom, and I certainly didn't want to fall flat on my face before I found my feet!

But then I came to realize a crucial lesson in my journey...

People will *always* have opinions; some may ridicule and laugh, while others will applaud my achievements. Regardless, in the end, *the only opinion that truly mattered was my own!* I am the one pursuing this dream, and my voice should be what matters most to me and my clients.

Following are some other key lessons I've learned along the way. My hope is that they will help you embark on your own journey to entrepreneurship.

**5 Lessons Learned by a Corporate Professional-Turned-Entrepreneur:**

1. **Have a Passion for Your Business Idea:** If you have a great idea you are passionate about, do your homework. Never let the thoughts of others prevent you from trying something different.

2. **Know Your Why:** Have a good reason (goal) for doing your business. Write it down on paper and review it frequently when times get tough along your journey. When you're committed to your why, you're unstoppable.

3. **Hire a Seasoned Coach:** Hire a coach who is tried and true. Research to ensure he or she has a track record of success. Check out that person's LinkedIn profiles and

Facebook pages. Ask key questions. There are a lot of "gurus" out there, and not all of them are reputable. Don't select someone blindly. Conduct your own background research, so you don't throw money at bad information and quickly go through your cash reserves.

4. **Eliminate Scarcity Mindset:** Don't make decisions when you are short on cash, as that is a scarcity mindset. When you are in business for yourself, there are no safety rails. You don't have a corporation behind you (unless you have investors). There are risks to your livelihood, home, bank accounts, and sometimes even your health. However, when you operate from a scarcity mindset, your negative thoughts are reflected in the universe and may become your reality. It's important to remember every business has its ups and downs when starting out. This is all a part of the journey of an entrepreneur. Stay the course and trust your instincts.

5. **Gratitude:** Give thanks every day. Be grateful for everything and everyone. Celebrate every win in your life.

**You CAN Have It All!** Believe in yourself and focus on the end goal. Yes, you will make mistakes along the way, but that is the beauty of your entrepreneurial journey—discovering the many facets and nuances of coming into your own is a wonderful experience.

Marion Segree is an experienced, results-driven IT professional and business coach with a successful online consulting practice. Her mission is to see the sparkle in her clients' eyes as they master the change within and realize how much they can accomplish outside a corporate role when they align their personal and business goals to become their own boss. You can learn more about her here: https://www.fromcorporatetoconsultant.com/.

Get Marion's free gift, a short video titled 5 Things You Can Do to Cope After a Layoff, here: https://hopebookseries.com/gifts/

# Chapter 9
## Don't Ever Give Up

By Carina Cheng Casuga

I have always yearned for a better life for my family. So, when we decided to migrate from the Philippines to Canada, it was to be a new and exciting adventure.

With a bachelor's degree in Medical Technology and management experience, I didn't anticipate much trouble in procuring a good job. Eventually, though, we found out that my degree was not easily transferable to Canada. To work in the field, I would have to take the whole program again. My husband and I had no choice but to start back at the bottom, taking jobs that paid minimum wage just to put food on the table. Clearly, it would not be enough to sustain a family of four.

I was so conflicted. As a mom, I wrestled with the guilt of losing valuable time with my family while working outside of the home to make ends meet. In addition, I missed the previous comforts of my home, familial surroundings, family, and friends.

I had left a well-paying management position only to end up doing tedious, boring tasks while being told what to do. I was struggling through a variety of personal, financial, emotional, spiritual, and health challenges (like migraines on average of five days a week), all of which were keeping me from living a fulfilling, peaceful life. And the hope of having that dream life was getting dimmer and dimmer.

I was overwhelmed, frustrated, alone, anxious, powerless, depressed, hopeless, disengaged, and finally, suicidal. I clearly remember the day; I took a handful of sleeping pills in the washroom, ready to leave this world. I was looking forward to not having to deal with all the issues and frustrations anymore. I honestly believed that, without me around, my husband and kids would for sure have a better life. (In case you didn't know or forgot, Christians are not exempt from hardships, sickness, insecurities, depression, and suicide.)

But, lo and behold, those handful of pills did not kill me. I woke up to my husband nursing me back to health. I was groggy for days, and remember thinking to myself (and being disappointed) that I couldn't even die right.

I was terrified of the idea that I had failed—that we would not have food and end up homeless. I then came across the following bible verse in Psalm 37:25:

*I was young and now I am old, yet I have never seen the righteous forsaken or their children begging bread.*

In the back of my mind, I figured God was not ready for me yet. I still had a part to play in the tapestry of my life. I had to dig deep, swallow my pride, *get up*, and try this thing called "life" again. And this time, I was going to give it all I had.

I prayed to God: "Since you are not ready for me yet, I will try again ... but this time, you have to be with me and give me strength."

I essentially made up my mind, resolved to the fact that the only way to overcome all of the challenges I was facing was through building strong spiritual, financial, educational, and family relationship as the foundation of everything.

So, while working a full-time job, I took financial, leadership, and management courses, which slowly took me from a sales representative at the local mall to a Global Payroll Manager of a mid-size company located downtown with a large window corner office that faces the mountains and sea.

As I progressed in my career, I also learned the value of emotional intelligence, growth mindset, and in partnering with the right people.

Now, 20 years later, I am the person I wished had been there for me when I was going through my struggles. I am now a speaker, founder of Star Life Consulting, author, personal development coach, and advocate for financial literary.

And I am passionate about helping others become better equipped to face life challenges without ever giving up!

I share my story to inspire and motivate others to develop, grow, and stay the course. At times, we all need to just stop and rest. That's okay! What's not okay is to allow yourself to get stuck, give in, or give up.

Rather, remember that there is *always* an alternative option, and you can always change your circumstances (financial, emotional, physical, etc.).

Perhaps most importantly, *you can always change your perspective.*

The most crucial mindset lesson I learned over the course of this journey is that success is subjective, relative, and time-based … which essentially means that there is no point in comparing myself to someone else. My success is authentically my own, relative to where I was before—and it's only temporary.

When I am going through and have to overcome a hurdle, it is time to look up, thank God, savor the moment, and get ready for the next success-story challenge. Purpose, happiness, and gratitude are intentional choices I have to make every single day;

without them, life has no essence. It would be the equivalent of breathing, but not being alive.

I opted for a growth mindset which enabled me to progress in all areas of my life, including how I manage, lead, parent, and show up in my relationships. Now, I'd like to share some of the mindset tools that literally saved my life, helped me move forward, and made life worth living.

**6 Essential Tools to Equip You to Live a More Fulfilled Life:**

1. **Seek Clarity.** Get clear on who, what, where, and why you want to be. Without clear purpose and direction, you are subject to your environment. Your purpose drives your resolve, which also helps you prioritize and facilitate decision making when considering opportunities. Consider the following questions: What is the vision you are moving toward? What role do you want to play—victor or victim? Who or what do you need to move toward your vision?

2. **Focus on Positive Perspective.** Your perspective determines your outcome. Happiness and success are conscious choices only you can make; no one can make them for you. Your resolve to have a positive perspective will boost your productivity, which leads to better results and less stress. Consider the following questions: What would it look like to succeed? What would it feel like? When you look back a year from now, what would you like to see?

3. **Keep Your Faith.** Your faith is fuel for your spirit and courage. Be honest and true about who, what, and why you believe, and it will carry you through the storms of life. Cultivate a strong relationship with the Lord; comprehend his character, principles, and will. Let your faith be evident and pure … make a solid choice you stand by no matter what. Consider the following questions: If I gave my God all my fear, doubt, troubles, and anger,

what would His response be? Who am I to God? Who am I trying to impress?

4. **Nurture Compassion.** Show kindness, thoughtfulness, forgiveness, and grace to yourself and others. Fully nourish and manage your physical, physiological, emotional, mental, spiritual, and relational needs. This has a direct impact on your well-being. If you don't take care of yourself, you won't be able to do anything you enjoy or set out to do. Make a conscious effort to disconnect with the negative and connect with love ones. Take some quiet time, appreciate, and be grateful. Breathe and rest!

5. **Invest in yourself.** Take the time to learn something new! Invest your time in improving yourself and circum stances. Take time to create and build something you have always wanted or enjoyed. Get further, faster, with a coach, mentor, partner, or team. Create effective partnerships and friendships that build you up and encourage you to do better.

6. **Save Money.** Save at least 10% of your income each pay period. Make sure you have an emergency fund with enough for at least three months. Learn about investing, tax free savings, government credits, and debt reduction. Find ways to have an additional income stream. You can't help anyone if you need money. Improving your financial wellness reduces stress, improves your relationships, and gives you the ability to help others. It also allows you to feel more in charge of your personal and financial situation. Understand and appreciate your source of income and revenue. Do not make the mistake of blaming someone or something else. YOU are fully accountable for your own life.

**You CAN Have It All!** As long as you still have breath in you, it is never too late to dream. You can make changes and live a more fulfilled life. Always remember that the outcome of your life is completely up to you; that is the gift of free will!

Decide how you want to paint the story of your life.

Carina Cheng Casuga is a results-driven professional who holds certifications in global payroll management, leadership, and personal development. Having overcome many challenges, from financial hardship to leading global teams, she advocates for financial literacy and personal development. A life-long learner who strives to continuously improve herself in her personal, professional, and spiritual life, she loves actively sharing and exchanging knowledge with her peer groups, students, and Christian-faith life groups. As a coach, speaker, and mentor, she provides a safe, confidential space to get clarity and actionable steps on achieving goals. You can learn more about her here: https://carinaspeaklife.com/.

**Get Carina's gift, a Financial Organizational Document, to better prepare for the unexpected, here: https://hope-bookseries.com/gifts/.**

# Chapter 10
## Be a Product of Your Expectations, Not Your Limitations

By Tamika L. Blythers

As an educator, I've sat through countless hours of hundreds of mind-numbing, unenthusiastic professional development presentations facilitated by consultants who were paid enormous amounts of money. Time and time again, they offered gray jargon replicated from other systems. Around late 2009, while listening to one such presenter, I couldn't help but wonder how long he had prepared, researched, and studied the subject matter, let alone practiced the presentation or finetuned his skills. After three long hours of twisting and turning in a plastic, unforgiving seat, I decided I could have conducted the same presentation in a more engaging manner.

Later that evening, attempting to anesthetize and wash away that three-hour tragedy, I binge- watched reruns of *Matlock*. While cross-examining a witness, Matlock posed the following question: "In my hand, I have a canceled check in the amount of $100,000 for consulting fees. What *were* you consulting about?" As the witness reluctantly shared an explanation, I inquisitively leaned in to analyze the response.

In that pivotal moment, my American Dream was debunked and challenged. It was no longer about a house in suburbia with a two-car garage, white picket fence, and two-point-five kids. The life-changing revelation hit me like a ton of bricks—my dream was to "be" a consultant ... hold up ... I *AM* a consultant!

Shifting my American Dream was challenging, because it went against everything I'd been taught and have heard.

But here's what I realized:

Somewhere along the way, the definition of a teacher, not to mention our duties and responsibilities, has been blurred. As in most things in life, I had choices in my profession—I could evangelize or antagonize, insult or inspire.

The gift and art of teaching navigated and catapulted me into several different professional arenas. It was through teaching that I decided to expand my zone of brilliance by empowering, educating, equipping, and encouraging others while incorporating practical, spiritually based solutions and inspirational personal experiences. This is how I became the blossoming hybrid I am today.

As an educator, I had been performing and perfecting my craft. After all, I had taught thousands of lessons and participated in and facilitated numerous trainings. For years, I've educated and equipped.

So, I stepped out of the classroom to launch my consulting business. Was it a leap of faith? Yes! Was I fearful? Yes! However, I did it despite the fear, and actually experienced a really smooth and seamless transition. Being an educator with a clear vision turned entrepreneur, I titled my consulting business Eduvizon. As a consultant, I solve problems and teach people in various circumstances how to define their lives with confidence and purpose.

It was during this time that I cashed in my teacher's retirement, invested in my dream, and toured with my first children's book, *Mika Dika Foster Kid*. There were so many shifts happening in my life that the need for "life balance" became very real to me. The more success a person attains, the more difficult it becomes to maintain a healthy balance. You definitely have to pick, choose, and refuse who and what gets your attention.

I started thinking about a formula for life's "Cycle of Balance," which of course has no perfect algorithm or unique design. But it became clear to me that the balance occurs according to how the nine points I identified are incorporated into your daily living.

These points provide realignment in a practical manner by refocusing and equipping in every aspect of our lives. This life-enhancing transformational tool I call "V.O.W. 9 Points of Impact" is designed to create and catapult "maintainable equilibrium" to the forefront while reintegrating "practice" into practical.

The nine points of impact work together as interconnected circles. If one circle is out of sync, then your entire balance is compromised. Think of it as a type of system that regulates your life, just as the nervous, circulatory, digestive, and other human body systems collaborate to regulate your body.

Those points of impact are: vision, voice, value, options, opportunities, obsessions, word, wisdom, and worship. Embedded in the V.O.W. 9 Points of Impact are three important goals: **Enlighten** to awaken and sharpen your insight, become **Empowered** to take action and be proactive, and be **Encouraged** to keep moving forward in perpetual progression.

Why are these goals important?

Let me ask you this:

Are you holding on to "good" when "greater" is waiting patiently just outside the room? Why are we faithful to the things that don't create a spark inside us—are they really that comfortable? By natural default, stagnation has major implications.

If you aspire to make a difference, shift your mindset from staying "safe" to taking a chance! Hold onto hope—the spark that ignites expectation and the desire for an expected result. A little hope makes you effective; a lot of hope makes you dangerous. Never relinquish your power. If you are afraid to soar, don't even bother spreading your wings. You will *always* rise to the level of your expectations.

Be a risk taker, rule breaker, deal maker, and game changer! Leave a legacy that resounds in the hearts of mankind. Once you've tasted excellence, the flavor of mediocrity will be unbearable, and you will be closer to having all you ever dreamed.

As a consultant, I enjoy providing insight to those blinded by limited experiences, exposures, and/or traumas. I know that one success, just one win, can propel them to the next level. My unquenchable thirst for change, growth, and happiness is my driving force. The "Why" that makes me cry at night is the sabotage and subterfuge many have chosen to accept rather than development and empowerment. Like an unwavering lotus, I provide a "clarion" call to action. What a gift, to give individuals hope and show them opportunity!

In my experience, I have seen many people lose faith in the idea of having everything they ever wanted in favor of being "safe." This results in numerous missed opportunities.

Which is why I'd like to offer the following tips, if you are ready to start chasing *your* American Dream—if you aspire to reach new heights—whatever that looks like for you:

**Tip 1: Focus on who *you* are.**

**Tip 2: Value what *you* bring to the table.**

**Tip 3: Master *your* craft and talents.**

**Tip 4: Realize that comparison is the thief of dreams.**

**Tip 5: Don't let fear stop you from making difficult decisions.**

**Tip 6: Seize EVERY opportunity.**

There's nothing more painful and disappointing as a "missed opportunity," especially when you come to realize that you didn't value the chance given. I am reminded of the man at the Pool of Bethesda, who wasted 38 years, I think due to lack of preparation and vision. The way you perceive an opportunity is in direct correlation to the intensity level of your pursuit.

When you're able to correctly differentiate a "Window of Opportunity" from a "Door of Opportunity," your perception is no longer distorted. There's a different draft and airflow that shifts the atmosphere when a door is opened as opposed to a window. Maturity and wisdom are required to appreciate the monumental magnitude of being given an opportunity. Study and calculate the cost before you find yourself being a victim of the 38-year "missed opportunity." Do not miss your moment!

I believe in my goals and dreams. I am a woman of influence because I have not only survived in the midst of insecurity, adversity, exploitation, and manipulation, but I've also thrived and persisted. I am impacting the world because I decided to come forth out of the cold, comfortable cave of confusion. I made a choice to use my gift of teaching as a tool of inspiration for others, and I found the life balance that is key to "having it all." My platform, plan, purpose, and position provide me with a life I could have never imagined.

So if you're ready to change your life, consider the tips above, and start taking action.

**You CAN Have It All!** To begin the journey, it only takes one thought, one decision, and one action. These three things can change the trajectory of a person's life forever, revolutionizing it!


Tamika L. Blythers is a dynamic educator, consultant, master trainer/facilitator, author, entrepreneur, host/emcee for conferences and events, and transformational speaker. Her platform, "V.O.W" 9 Points of Impact, is a simple shared message of self-inquiry which requires individuals to radically change perspectives about their decisions and goals in life. You can learn more about her here: https://www.upperroomwriter.com.

**Get T.L.'s free gift, her 5 Principles to Transform Your Life's Landscape, here: https://hopebookseries.com/gifts/.**

# Chapter 11

## The Magic to Creating Anything:
## 4 Steps to Manifesting Your Dream

*By Dr. Angelica Benavides*

My journey to motherhood began in 1985. I saw many doctors and tried everything you can think of to conceive … even the most unusual remedies in Western Medicine (think head standing immediately after sex, which, by the way, is NOT a proven aid in conception).

I learned about family planning (aka fertility awareness) and tracked fertility signs. I took my temperature in the morning every day and before going to bed, completed a cervical mucus check, and charted my menstrual cycle on a calendar for years. Every time the signs were present, I would call my husband so he would drop everything and run home to have sex. I admit that we took the passion and fun out of having sex. Our focus was to get pregnant, and honestly, it ruined our sex, intimacy, and connection.

I tried everything, but nothing worked for me.

For almost eight years, I cried almost every night, and I prayed. I also truly felt my prayers went unanswered.

I often wondered if I'd done something wrong in life, or if maybe I was paying some sort of karmic debt. I wondered why so many other women could get pregnant, many of whom didn't even desire their pregnancy or child. And there I was, in deep sadness, because despite all my efforts, I had such trouble conceiving. And when I did conceive, I miscarried.

One day, lost in sorrow, I visited a spiritual teacher who I admire dearly. I cried as I told him how I felt everyone else seemed to deserve a child except me. He looked at me with great conviction and said, "You have the power to get pregnant … if you believe."

Then, he asked me: "Do you believe you can get pregnant?"

In shock, I looked at him and replied, "I have tried everything within my power. What do you mean, 'if I believe,' I can get pregnant?"

He told me to follow four specific steps without fail to achieve whatever I desired. Warning me of the inner voice that *would* try to derail me from my beliefs that I *can* get pregnant, he reiterated again: "You *have* to believe." I questioned him further. "But I've tried everything."

He heard the great doubt and uncertainty in my voice and said, "If you can't believe, I can't reveal the secret. You must believe first! Do you believe?" he asked again.

"But Father," I said, "I've already tried everything!"

Clearly disappointed, he said, "Forget it. You have to go now. I don't want to waste my time."

Something clicked, and I said, "Okay! I believe I can get pregnant! Please tell me what to do."

And then, he shared the powerful secret that completely changed my life—the four steps to manifesting.

"First, you have to believe you can achieve anything," he said again.

"Second, practice grace. You and your husband will come here every day for nine weeks to practice grace. You don't have to go to a parish or church, but you will create a daily ritual where you practice grace.

"Third, you must create awareness. Capture your inner voice.

"Finally, regardless of what that voice tells you and what you've seen or are seeing, practice the following phrase to tap into belief vibration (or energy thought process): 'What if I can get …'"

When my spiritual teacher shared these four secrets, I went home to share them with my husband. We both went to mass without questioning and attended every day with the intention of being thankful to God for allowing us to have our miracle baby. The more we went, and the more we practiced grace, the more we truly began to believe I was pregnant. One day, after only six weeks of practicing the four secret steps, I missed my period. Before taking the pregnancy test, I envisioned myself celebrating the positive results. As soon as I saw the pregnancy results, I cried from happiness. I called my whole family and danced with joy. I immediately went to my spiritual teacher and held him tight, and we cried together in joy! He looked at me and said, "You must remember to simply *believe* that you can achieve anything."

Here's what I have learned from my experience with the four steps: I believe I can achieve anything. I was able to get pregnant in six weeks after having tried everything else under the sun for more than eight years. I was happily pregnant and had the most beautiful baby boy!

The truth is, *the magic to creating anything you want exists within you*. You must be in alignment with your thoughts, beliefs, and emotions, and practice grace on a daily basis in order to tap into the Magic of Creation. You *can* achieve anything.

When we struggle to manifest our heart's desire, it is often because we don't have clarity on what we truly want. For instance, I could not see myself pregnant until I started practicing grace; then, I could see myself in maternity clothes. I even remember how I had questioned myself while going to the university, asking, "Do I *really* want to get pregnant?"

In order to manifest what you want, you must be certain that you really want to achieve your goal.

Another reason we struggle to manifest is because our beliefs are not in alignment with our desires. Our heart desires the dream, but our thoughts remind us why we can't have it. This inner voice (aka "monkey-mind chatter") is present in all of us, and we tend to truly believe it. It gets in the way of our achieving goals. Buddhists define this voice as "unsettled, restless, capricious, whimsical, fanciful inconstant, confused, indecisive, an uncontrollable."

Where does this often-self-sabotaging inner voice come from? Our early life experiences. We internalize them, and then, adopt them into our beliefs about ourselves. They come from our parents, grandparents, teachers, and/or early caregivers, and they are comprised of thoughts, beliefs, and attitudes that generally oppose our best interests and diminish our self-esteem.

It is also quite difficult to stay positive while waiting for what we want so badly.

Even worse, some of us don't even dare to dream at all, because we don't feel we *deserve* it—we aren't worthy.

The great news is that we *all* have the power to change our brain. *The idea is to transform your limiting beliefs into those that support your goal or heart's desire.* Let's go back to the four steps I learned that day, when I went to see my spiritual mentor.

**Step 1: Believe you can achieve anything.** Pay attention to your thoughts and feelings. When you truly begin to believe, take notice of the positive feelings that begin bubbling up. When negative feelings and thoughts come to you (and they will—remember, this is a "practice"), make the conscious choice to not allow them to control your reality. Change them to positive beliefs. (If you are struggling to truly believe, look for evidence around you of someone who has achieved what you desire. Remember Roger Bannister? He ran the four-minute mile, which was thought "impossible" by "informed" observers. Roger had the "breaking" belief that it could be done, and others followed.) Paying attention to your thoughts and beliefs in this manner will help re-shape your brain and experience.

**Step 2: Practice Grace.** Practicing grace is the most difficult step of them all. Find things or surround yourself with beautiful things you love and feel grateful for. Practice meditation and focus on your breath when your mind demands what you desire (and see no evidence of) in your present life experience. Go to a lake or garden, pet a dog, or find something that will distract the mind from hoping and wishing to have your heart's desire now.

**Step 3: Create Awareness.** Being aware of your daily thoughts is vital. Learn to shift your focus if it doesn't support your heart's desires. The Law of Focus states that whatever we focus on, we become better at, and eventually become. What do you want to become or be better at? Old beliefs are lies your brain is telling you about who you can become or are. Choose to create new beliefs, which align with your heart's desire.

**Step 4: Practice the Phrase, "What If I Can Get ..."** Repeating this phrase softens the negative chatter from your inner voice and shifts your mindset to the possibilities available to you to achieve what you desire. It's considered a positive affirmation, which is *so* powerful, because it releases you from the inner chatter and negative fear, worry, and/or anxiety. Affirmations begin to take charge of your thoughts, slowly, and ultimately change your pattern of thinking. Remember, what you focus on is what becomes powerful in your life.

Having used these four steps to achieve my dream of becoming a mother, I then chose to follow the path of being a transformational leader who inspires others to reach beyond their perceived capabilities, unleash their superpowers, and turn their dreams into reality. I love helping people break through limiting beliefs, emotions, and patterns that limit them from doing, being, and achieving what their heart desires.

As an Intuitive Coach, I practice clinical hypnosis and NLP to help people dive deep into understanding their archetypal patterns, past lives, shadow side, and birth/childhood issues, and increase their energetic vibration, so they can transform their lives and achieve their greatest goals.

My life and soul purpose is helping others discover their higher self—and I absolutely love what I do!

**You CAN Have It All!** If you believe, create a daily routine of practicing grace, cultivate awareness, and recite affirmations, something amazing happens inside you! You begin to create magic by design instead of by accident. You experience changes in the brain, which *is* malleable. It shapes who you are and what you can become. Most importantly, it is responsible for what you can achieve in your life.


Dr. Angelica Benavides is an influential leader and human learning expert with a unique ability to help people release the mental obstacles that prevent them from achieving their very best at work, in business, and in life. Committed to empowering others to exchange the chaos of life for the best life possible, she is a recognized authority on the psychology of leadership and peak performance. She has appeared on Daytime National TV, NBC, and Fox, and is an international speaker, co-publisher, and founder of Empresarios LatinX and the Master Manifestor Lab. You can learn more about her here: https://drb.groovepages.com/consciousmanifestation/.

**Get Dr. Angelica's free gift, a Unlock Your Full Potential Free Coaching Session to manifest what you really want, here: https://hopebookseries.com/gifts/.**

# Chapter 12

## Getting on the Road to Your Dream Life

By Anastasiya Bezugla

The biggest gift we all share is the ability to tap freely into our imagination. You can close your eyes at any given moment and create an image that will be unique, personal, and true to you. Doing so allows you to explore the wildest, untamed, up-lifting, and exhilarating experiences. Your imagination does not care about your financial or social status; it does not require you to have formal education; it does not judge. It's non-resistant.

Sometimes, it may feel silly to allow yourself to dream your biggest dreams. The older we get, the less importance we tend to place on our imagination and its abilities. We tend to disconnect from its power, but it is always there, whispering softly to you. As APJ Abdul Kalam said, "You have to dream before your dreams can come true."

Think back to when you were a child. Did you have a dream that sparked joy in every cell of your body? Perhaps you wanted to become a doctor, or lawyer, or veterinarian. Maybe you dreamed about helping the world or climbing a mountain. We all had our fantasies.

When I was growing up in a small, rural town in Ukraine, I dreamed about seeing the world. At the time, the chances of that happening were freakishly small, since my parents could barely provide food for the table. When I was in sixth grade, our school introduced English as second language. I remember struggling with the alphabet, grammar, and correct pronunciation, but I fell in love with the culture and traditions. I could see myself living in America someday, and became obsessed with my new English class.

When I was in seventh grade, I had a dream. I was standing by the airplane that was about to take me to America. The access to the gate was slick and difficult to approach, but the desire to board the plane was significant. The dream ended with me flying through the sky on my way to my dream life. I woke up feeling anxious, nervous, and excited.

My fixation with the culture of the USA continued throughout my school years. I practiced English in front of the mirror and watched movies. At the beginning of my fourth year in the University, I was looking for a job when I saw an ad about a work-and-travel opportunity in the United States. It took me one year to figure out the financial aspect—and to get my parents' permission—to go. Finally, on May 25th, 2006, just as I had in my dream, I boarded a plane that would take me to the place that I had been imagining since the sixth grade.

I have lived in the United States ever since. Even though I left my family and friends and had to completely start over in a different country, I have always felt confident about my decision and never looked back. To this day, when I lose sight of the power of imagination, I remind myself that anything is possible. Our dreams are *meant* to come true, and if we believe in them, they will.

It's human nature to strive for a better life filled with abundance. Many times, we experience a gap between where we are now and where we want to be. Some days, it seems impossible to move forward, so it's easy to give up. Think about everything you've said you are going to do but never did. Think of all the ideas that ran through your head that you dismissed. In the end, we feel sorry for ourselves. The victim mode kicks in, and the guilt, pressure, and overall anger with yourself reflects on everything you are and do. You end up blaming the world around you, not because you are a mean person, but because you are scared and doubtful.

I have been there. There was a period in my life when I felt sorry for myself every day. I was in a complete denial of the fact that *I* am in charge of my life. I had severe anxiety and panic attacks that disrupted my daily life. I would stumble out of bed in the morning without any goals or visions. I told myself that I am not good enough, smart enough, pretty enough. I did not like me. I did not see myself as a strong woman who can achieve things. I guilt-tripped myself about things I did not do. My self-talk got so bad at one point that I questioned my whole existence.

I remember the day I became trapped in my car in the emergency lane because I couldn't drive. The panic attack made me dizzy, and my heart was about to jump out of my chest. I remember being absolutely lost in my thoughts. In that moment, I realized I had no vision of what is next for me. All I knew was that I wanted to change.

And I became aware of another simple truth: in order to get to a different place, you need a clear vision and basic directions.

Think about it. If you decided to go to a new destination, but you didn't know the name of the place, which route to take, or what to pack, do you think you would make it there?

I believe every human being on this planet can create the life he or she desires, fulfill his/her purpose, and enjoy the manifestation of dreams. It is not about where you come from or where you have been.

*It's about where you are going.*

Progress equals happiness.

The main reason people live without a true purpose is because they simply do not know where to go.

If you can relate, the following tips will help you find your sense of direction, and hopefully, get you on your way to where you probably should have been a long time ago.

### Tip 1. The power of visualization.

What you think, you become.

There are many scientific studies that prove it. The more you visualize a specific goal, the clearer the outcome will be. You can manifest anything you like, and there is no limit. How is that for a power?

When I was in my early twenties, I was a 'starving' student with no money, but I wanted to travel. I was studying hospitality management, and one of the requirements was to attend a yearly tourism expo. These expos distribute tons of brochures featuring colorful and exotic destinations. When I got home that evening, my heart was aching to travel. I looked through the brochures longingly, and then, I drew myself swimming in the pool at Hilton Waterfall resort at the sunny Sharm El Sheikh Egypt. I visualized enjoying the sun on my skin, savoring delicious fruit, and swimming. Exactly a year later, I was swimming in the pool at the Sharm El Sheikh Holiday Inn all-inclusive resort with my friends. The resort I had drawn was only a mile away. Coincidence? I don't think so! And I still have the brochure to prove it.

I have visualized my dream home, the car I am now driving, my entire professional career … even my two dogs! And I know that, as long as I practice the power of visualization, I can have anything I want.

*The key here is to focus on the details when you are visualizing, and 'experience' it as if it is actually happening in that moment.*

### Tip 2: The Power of Mindset.

Train your mind.

Mindset is all about the ways you perceive all your life's experiences. Your attitude determines your altitude.

I believe we all born the same—not in the same circumstances, no. But we are all wired the same. So, being treated like the queen of the castle when you were a child does not guarantee your being set for life. Vice versa, coming from humble beginnings does not automatically land you in the struggle zone indefinitely.

We all have a choice. You can choose to train your mind and create new habits that will bring you closer to the life you desire, or you can accept the possibility of maybe never realizing your dream.

Think of your mindset as a well-oiled engine of a car. You choose a destination, and you have directions, but your engine will not start. In order to stay on the road, you will need a strong motor that can help you overcome detours and construction on the road.

*Your mindset is the powerful engine of your life.*

Luckily, there are many ways you can start today to change your mindset, and none of them require complicated rules or financial obligations. All you have to do is make the choice to move forward toward the life that you desire, so you can finally live it!

### Tip 3: The Power of Action.

Close the gap.

So, now you have a map to your destination (visualization), and your car engine is running smooth and strong (mindset).

Now, you drive.

If you don't drive the car every single day toward your destination, but instead sit in the parking lot *thinking* about your lost dreams, you will still be exactly where you are now. You must take consistent action toward your goals. You do not build an empire in a week. You do not build it in a month. You build it day by day, as long as it takes.

The problem is, so many people are too *scared* to take action ... especially the ones that matter most. The reason? The fear of failure. We think that we are not smart enough, old enough, young enough, business savvy enough. The fear keeps us from shifting gears to *move*.

Making any steps, big or small, toward your dream is the power of action. Any beginning requires patience, action, and the ability to see the bigger picture. You almost never know exactly what do to at the beginning, but by making small steps and learning as you go, you are bound to succeed. In fact, here's another lesson I've learned:

*If you're scared, then it's a must.*

We often go through life underestimating how much time we have. My message to you is that your tomorrow is what you make today! Taking risks in your life and building your life around your desires sounds terrifying and overwhelming, I know. But it's also exhilarating, and *so* worth it.

**You CAN Have It All!** Your dreams *can* come true. Keep your focus on what matter most to you: financial freedom, more family time, traveling the world, buying your dream home, building a business ... whatever it is. Be hungry for change, and become obsessed with your vision. Let go of the fear that life has limited resources. The Universe is abundant, and it's always on your side. Do not worry about things that could go wrong, and start concentrating on the things that can go so beautifully right.

You are worthy of the very best that life has to offer. So love yourself enough to go after what you want! Your dreams matter; your goals matter; you matter. With gratitude in your heart and the hunger for change in your soul, you can make all your dreams come true.

Anastasiya Bezugla is a Ukrainian living her dream in the USA. Born to inspire others to go after their dreams, she is the queen of never giving up. A successful online business entrepreneur, she is also a lifelong believer in the phrase, "Mindset matters," and teaches others how to harness the power of mindset (she's a veteran of two Unleash the Power Within Tony Robbins live events) and other LOA techniques via her blog, Mindset Chick. She is also a wife and mother. You can learn more about her by following her here: https://www.mindsetchick.net/.

**Get Anastasiya's free gift, Close the Gap, to discover what is stopping you from accomplishing your biggest goals here: https://hopebookseries.com/gifts/.**

# Chapter 13

## Walking Like an Egyptian

By Heidi Albarbary

"What more can you have?" asked a friend. "You are successful in your career. You hold a prestigious position many would love to trade places with you to have …"

Her words stuck in my mind for so long!

She was right. I could see how people around me seemed to envy me, and I could understand why. Yet, despite having achieved so much in my professional career, I felt unfulfilled. It wasn't my dream job, nor was I living my dream life. I knew I didn't want to go through my entire existence doing what I was doing.

In truth, I had a completely different vision for myself.

Growing up in Egypt and Kuwait, I was raised by parents who valued tradition. They also had high expectations of their daughter. Since the age of 15, I was acutely aware of the oppression of women in a male-oriented culture despite their potential. It instilled a dream in me; I wanted to break ground as a successful woman in the MENA region. In pursuit of that dream, I would become an advocate for female entrepreneurship ... I would be a woman of influence who would not allow anyone to define me in a society that is still overwhelmingly male dominated!

And so, in 2004, after graduating from university with honors in the top five of my class, I was offered the opportunity to become a teacher's assistant at one of the reputable universities in Cairo, Egypt, teaching subjects in my field of study, Business Administration. Considering that it is one of the most prestigious positions any university graduate can acquire, I seized the valuable opportunity.

No, it was not my dream job! Nevertheless, I thought it would be worthwhile to work, and hoped it might turn into a valuable steppingstone while I pursued my master's degree in Business Administration (which I had started immediately after receiving my bachelor's).

I worked tirelessly to finalize my thesis and earn my master's degree, and after two years of hard work and research, managing my time between my job at the university and my studies as a master's student, I finally graduated in 2007!

I was offered an entry-level position in an advertising agency, and not just any agency, but the best in the business—the leader in the Egyptian advertising industry. It was a challenging decision, and no one believed I would go for it. But, because I was not fond of being a teacher's assistant, nor was it a career path I had really wanted in the first place, I decided to take the position with the agency, starting at the very bottom of the ladder.

There I was, starting a brand-new career path. I was determined to climb the ladder at an incredible pace, and I did ... receiving four promotions to different levels in a timespan of less than three years! It wasn't easy. This was not a job where 9-5 would cut it—eight hours simply wasn't enough to finish my tasks. I got used to 12-15-hour workdays, six days a week. With barely any time left over for a social life, everything revolved around my work.

In short, I turned into a workaholic.

When I became aware of this fact, I tried so hard to balance my life again: regain focus of my vision, what matters, and time management. I started to squeeze in some "me" time, socializing with old friends once again. I also re-connected with an old friend whom I had lost contact with for almost six years. We remained in touch, and our friendship grew until ... it was love! He proposed in 2009, and I was soon to be married.

My life began to take a different shape. I was finally able to gain some balance, even though work still occupied the biggest portion of my time. Soon, though, I began feeling like "some" balance wasn't enough. I wasn't fulfilling a dream, and I had no time for anything else. It was time to leave my corporate job and start focusing on what really mattered to me.

And that's what I did.

On the same day I officially quit, I received a phone call from a client whose account I had been handling at the agency. He told me they had been headhunting me for more than two years! When they heard I had left my position at the agency, they decided to offer me a supervisory position at their organization, no interview required. The job was mine, and my office was ready.

The only problem? My wedding was only a month away, and I was reluctant to take a new position just to turn around to leave for a honeymoon after starting. They extended their offer to work around my personal schedule. I did not know what to expect, but I was willing to take the opportunity and explore a new experience. I signed the agreement.

I was in a phase of change! I got married and started my new corporate position. I also became pregnant just a few months after taking the job. To add to all this, an unprecedented Egyptian Revolution spread across the country causing mayhem and economic downfall.

It was overwhelming, and I struggled for many years afterward trying to regain balance in my life once again. It certainly was not easy, but my positive outlook became the light at the end of my tunnel, always guiding me. I was determined to reach my ultimate vision of advocating for female entrepreneurship no matter how long it took, regardless of the obstacles I was facing and everything happening around me.

I knew drastic change requires drastic measures. I would have to do something big (and different!) to follow my dreams. It took a ton of courage, but my family and I decided to start a new chapter in our life.

In 2018, I left my family and life in Egypt behind to build a new life in a foreign land of dreams. I moved to Canada with my then six-year-old son and nothing but our suitcases. This brand-new journey meant starting from scratch in a world of opportunities, and the excitement was rising … along with the fear.

I had a plan. It was not *crystal* clear, but my mindset was powerful enough to keep me going, and I was filled with optimism.

I was also going into this new journey with "eyes wide open," so to speak. I had been advised that, without any "Canadian" work experience, I would likely not be able to find a job easily. I knew I would probably have to start with a "survival job" just to put food on the table. While I was up to the challenge and ready for whatever life would throw at me, I still maintained positivity, searching for jobs that fit my work experience from back home. Not so surprisingly, I landed a job in my field of experience after only two months of searching! And I managed to establish a life for myself and my family.

Things were going well—so well, in fact, that I came to a "knowing": it was finally time to pursue my "real" dream. I was determined to start my very own business and become a well-known, successful business mentor and coach whose mission was to inspire women to be more than they thought they could be. I was driven to make a positive contribution to others with my life experience—to help them build wealth while growing into the people I knew they could be. I wanted to help them grow internally while living their absolute best life, fully embracing and enjoying love, family, and their dreams.

Today, I am living my dream as a proud business professional and *mompreneur*! I mentor women all around the world, guiding them through the process of building an online business of their own and leveraging the digital world.

Here's what I learned:

Life is not perfect. "Perfection" is *not* the key to having it all! It's all about your mindset. Having an abundance mindset means you are optimistic about the future; you are confident that things will work out despite the inevitable bumps in the road along the way.

The key: make decisions based on the big picture rather than a single snapshot in time.

*When you embody this mindset, you stop making excuses, realize your potential, attract opportunity, and commit to living your dreams!*

My life's path has not been smooth, but I am so grateful for it! It taught me a vital lesson, one that helped me liberate myself from a job and lifestyle that didn't fulfill my dream. It (eventually) brought me to where I am now—living my dream!

The experience of being an entrepreneur changes you fundamentally: from the way you think to the way you act and live your life. Most of the time, those changes are for the better.

Throughout my journey, I became aware of the fact that successful women entrepreneurs are all very different, even if they work in the same field. Nevertheless, there are specific traits that they all seem to embody in some way.

To that end, I'd like to share with you my …

**Top 15 Steps to Become a Successful Woman Entrepreneur:**

1. Set a determined and clear goal and be ruthless in achieving it.

2. Begin every day with a purpose.

3. Believe in yourself.

4. Accept failure wholeheartedly, and don't be afraid of it (because you *will* experience it).

5. Avoid negative people at all costs, and get rid of anything in your life that doesn't serve you.

6. Learn how to say "no" without feeling guilty.

7. Work *smarter*, not harder.

8. Don't be afraid to defy conventional methods.

9. Make trying new things a habit—don't ever let fear stop you.

10. Build a network.

11. Manage your time effectively, and be disciplined about your "me" time.

12. Be grateful (gratitude is a powerful component of the Law of Attraction).

13. Be confident.

14. Maintain a positive mindset.

15. Embrace what life is trying to teach you!

My advice: Reach for your *dream*, and believe you *will* achieve it. Consider opportunities not as challenges that might result in failure, but as proof of the potential you have that others see so clearly.

According to Forbes, women started an average of 1,821 new businesses per day in the U.S between 2017 and 2018, and they now make up a whopping 40% of new entrepreneurs! More women are turning to entrepreneurship than ever before. YOU can be one of them … and when you choose this road, you choose the path that can really take you to your dream life.

**You CAN Have It All!** Believe in that! Women are so powerful. Take pride in yourself and embrace your authenticity. You *are* an influencer; all you need to do is to bring it out of yourself and let it shine!

Heidi Albarbary is the Founder and CEO of HEIDI et Heidar Marketing. A creative visionary, and modern-day *mompreneur* all the way from Egypt—land of the Pharaohs—to Toronto, Canada, she has a master's degree in Business Administration and another in Business Psychology from the University of South Wales. Heidi's mission is to become one of the most prominent online business mentors for a generation of women seeking ownership of their careers and futures. You can learn more about her here: https://www.heidietheidarlive.com/.

**Get Heidi's gift to you, her 90-minutes on-demand workshop, How to Run A Digital Business From Your Kitchen, to learn how to leverage the online space as an entrepreneur, here: https://hopebookseries.com/gifts/.**

# Chapter 14

## You Must Try Again: A Different Perspective on Failure

By Sonia Michelle Reynolds

As a child, I remember struggling to get to sleep as my mother worked on an industrial sewing machine well into the night. There it sat in the corner of the room I shared with my sisters, the loud noise literally vibrating the entire house. Nurse by day, machinist by night, my mother worked hard and long to contribute to the family income. My father, a bricklayer by trade, would take the wool sweaters she made and sell them to his fellow colleagues on the building site.

My parents were Windrush immigrants in the 1960's, traveling from sunny Jamaica to England. Working evenings in addition to a day job was the normality for many West Indian families just to keep a home. When I look back now, it amazes me how, while once an irritation, the sewing machine became my ultimate interest.

At the age of nine, I begged my mother to teach me to sew. Her response was to hand me the painstaking task of stitching (without thread) on a sheet of writing paper. The joy I felt when I could finally move down the lines of punched holes in a perfect trail with the needle was immense! I knew that accomplishment meant I could 'graduate' to using actual thread and material, and I was so excited! Maybe it was the conversation I overheard between my parents as my father relayed the gratitude his fellow workmates felt toward my mother for the sweaters that sparked my desire to work in clothing—to ultimately become a fashion designer. "Make clothes, make people happy" was my interpretation of the situation around me.

So for the next fourteen years, I underwent a journey full of highs and lows before graduating with a textile degree.

I then worked as an overseas intern at a company called Old Glory in the USA. I fell in love with all areas of knitwear manufacturing, so I decided to start my own business, Sonia Michelle Exclusive Quality Knitwear! I quickly began attracting the attention of the media, selling sample designs globally to top fashion houses such as Donna Karan NY. Orders were coming in from boutiques near and far … Spain, USA, London, and I literally felt the world was my oyster. I married four years later, and with a whirlwind new life, failed to notice the slowing of incoming orders.

Watching the local news one evening, I saw that a large retailer had decided to take its manufacturing overseas to survive increasing costs of sourcing locally. It never dawned on me that my customers would do the same. I still remember the call from one of the few remaining boutiques I supplied, letting me know that they could now import similar-quality products at a much lower rate. At the time, I was also experiencing ill health connected with the pregnancy of my second child.

Do you know what it's like to spend years building something only to see it disappear in a moment? I was shattered, watching my lifelong dream crumble. I comforted myself with the thought, *"I will start again."* Then, I experienced the reality that millions of us experience every day: the demands of a young family made it impossible for me to really entertain the notion of restarting. I can still hear my inner voice telling me to stop dreaming!

I loved my family, but the meaning and purpose I felt while pursuing my design career just wouldn't go away... and I didn't want it to. I knew then that, in order to resurrect my business, I had to do something! But how? With zero free time and zero funds, it seemed impossible.

I'm not sure when I first became aware of a little book called *As a Man Thinketh* by James Allen, but I remember what I learned from it: I am a product of my thoughts. Contemplating the "What can I do?" question over and over again, my mind was filled with negativity, which just wasn't me. I considered myself a positive person ... a woman of faith, and a seasoned entrepreneur! Had the loss of my first business changed me so much? Had the added responsibility of a young family somehow made me extremely cautious and fearful?

The inner voice was loud:

*What if I tried something new and failed?*

*How could I sacrifice the time I should be spending with my family?*

*What if the market I was entering changed again, and I ended up with a huge debt?*

*What if people I knew from my other business saw me trying another one; would they laugh?*

The fears that pop up when we pursue a life change are endless. We *all* have doubts. Some of us also maintain the deep feeling inside ourselves that change *is* possible, if only we had direction.

I knew I needed more than thinking—something more than a motivational story. I needed something to speak directly to me that would give me the confidence to implement. At that point, I remember thinking about my children, and how they dealt with transition. In their early life, they repeatedly adapted to deal with change associated with natural growth.

I to put pen to paper and wrote:

*When a child is learning to walk, he or she will fall down many times, yet his natural instinct is to get up and try again. This action is not taught; it is something deep within them. Every failed attempt to walk is disregarded by loving parents or guardians while every effort often rewarded with praise. Just as it is in childhood, so it should be in adulthood! When striving to achieve something, failed attempts should be brushed off, while every effort to attain should be encouraged with praise. Individuals are rewarded for their achievements and not for the mistakes or failures they may have made on their journey to success. The event of a failure is irrelevant and impersonal, because it is an inevitable part of any learning process. Therefore, when pursuing your goal, it is not the failure that should be focused on. Instead, it is vitally important to take note of the lessons learned from the failed event **and move on**.*

So many entrepreneurs face failure on their journeys to success. Bill Gates was a university dropout before he went on the establish Microsoft! Thomas Alva Edison had over 1,000 registered patents, hundreds of them failing to attract any interest, yet his invention of the lightbulb continues to have a massive impact on life today. These individuals refused to allow earlier failures, conflict, defeat, pain, embarrassment, or negativity to hijack their dreams!

People often believe that "high achievers" possess unique qualities. The truth is, we are all born with an innate ability to keep trying until we succeed; it's simply our choice whether we do or not. Just as we are all born with the five senses—sight, touch, hearing, smell, and taste—we are also all born with five character traits: tenacity, determination, adaptability, discipline, and endurance. And just as one or more of our five senses can be deficient, underdeveloped, or completely inactive, the same goes with our five character traits.

The bottom line is, *your mindset determines your decisions.*

Viewing negative experiences through a new lens can make all the difference. When we sincerely embrace the notion that we all have the ability within us to obtain and achieve great things, we will make the decision to keep going until we do.

My best piece of advice when it comes to harnessing the power of your mind to achieve your dreams is to embrace the fact that, if others have done it, *so can you*.

Here's how to get started:

**Step 1: Get clear on what you want to achieve.** What does your ideal life look like? Set aside all limited thinking—quiet all the voices that raise all the fears, and describe your perfect day in writing. What purpose or passion are you undertaking?

**Step 2: List every fear or barrier keeping you from achieving what you want.**

**Step 3: Counter each and every fear with a positive solution (again, in writing).** If you can't think of a solution, try Googling it (i.e., "How to get over…"; "How to obtain").

Once you have completed these three steps, you will see that there are *always* solutions to the barriers keeping you from obtaining your goals.

When I finally came to understand the importance of mindset, and I began using tools like the exercise I just shared with you above, everything changed!

Drawing on my design skills and new mindset knowledge, I purchased a small real estate investment property with a conventional loan from the bank. Having done my research, I made 40,000 in 90 days as a newbie investor! Fast forward 24 months, and I had achieved a seven-figure asset base. That allowed me to revitalize my business in textiles without the financial pressure. And since then, my design work has gone on to win awards and is currently listed in the UPENN Fisher Arts Gallery.

I thank God for the simple tools I have used to move from motivation to implementation.

If you are also struggling to take action on your dreams, please know you are not alone! Consider the following women who have obtained their heart's desires, irrespective of obstacles:

Oprah Winfrey was born in 1954 in a small farming community in Mississippi. She suffered sexual abuse from a number of male relatives and friends of her mother. According to the *Forbes International* "rich list," Oprah is the only black billionaire in the world for three straight years.

Agatha Christie, born 15 September 1890, was the world's bestselling book writer of all time. Only truly surpassed by the Bible, her books sold approximately four billion copies worldwide. Agatha suffered from dyslexia, but it did not stop her from being creative and learning how to write.

Elizabeth Fry, born 21 May 1780, was a major driving force behind new legislation to make the treatment of prisoners more humane. From 2002 to 2015, her image has been depicted on the Bank of England £5 note. As the mother of eleven children, Elizabeth had limited time to dedicate to her passion, but she found a way.

Margaret Hilda Thatcher (Baroness Thatcher) born 25 October 1925, is a former British politician who served as Prime Minister of the United Kingdom from 1979 to 1990. She qualified as a barrister in 1953 specialising in tax law. In the same year, her twin children Carol and Mark were born.

The truth is, **You CAN Have It All!** Instead of allowing obstacles and failures to cause us to stop trying—to give up—perhaps they can ignite an emotion in us that builds fierce determination!


Sonia Michelle Reynolds is the inventor of the Award-winning textile Zephlinear™ and a women's business/life coach. Sonia's other business interests include real estate and publishing. A recipient of the community champions award for a project that supported over 4000 families, Sonia is currently finalising her Ph.D. while offering online courses and presenting at speaking engagements. You can learn more about her here: https://visionmadevisual.com/about-sonia/.

**Get Sonia's gift, her Talent & Skills Toolkit, designed to help you shed light on the unique offerings you have to share with the world, here: https://hopebookseries.com/gifts/.**

# Chapter 15

## Self-Image Dictates Your Environment and Results

*By Petra Buric*

Do you ever ask yourself, *"Is this all there is to get out of my life?"*

In the past, I had never thought of that question … until 2016. Up until then, it seemed I was simply following a predestined path set out before me. I had a job. Then, I tried entrepreneurship. I went on holidays maybe twice a year and completed my various chores. But I felt like I was trapped in a matrix of absolute mediocrity.

I was repeating the exact life of my parents (horror!): enough income to barely get by, debts, and no bright future. I didn't particularly like it, but I also had no idea how to get out of it. I accepted being born into it … it was just a "given" to live the way I was. I noticed beautiful people around me enjoying different, fabulous, more fulfilled, better lives than I, and I wondered how it was possible. Why did they "make it," when I hadn't?

Looking back, I now know that I had been too lazy mentally to find the answer to that puzzle. I was in full grip of my comfort zone without even realizing it.

The summer of 2011 brought about some changes. I moved from my home country to Switzerland, learned a totally new language, got a job, and a year later, I got married. But after these changes settled, the rut came back—that same "I'm-stuck-with-this" feeling. I needed to change something, but I didn't know what or how. I came to realize that despite the changes I *had* made, I was not growing.

What I didn't know at that time was that *I was supposed to choose growth on purpose by initiating a different type of change.*

In 2014, fed up with feeling stuck, I decided to DO something about it. I figured out that, if I improved my education, I'd probably get a better job with more income. Since I already had a university degree, I thought the next logical step was a master's. Full of hope, I attended a business school fair to find the one for me.

The message I received, though, was that since I was not a business owner, manager, or leader ... since I had not studied economics ... or business ... or anything particularly "significant," I was not good enough! I left disappointed.

Some days later, a recruiter from a business school in London, UK, contacted me saying my LinkedIn profile looked interesting, and I should start the application process. I literally had no idea what it meant, but I was intrigued, and I jumped in without thinking twice! While submitting the piles of documents required, I never really believed I'd actually be admitted.

So when the news came, it was absolutely unexpected! The recruiter called me and congratulated me for my acceptance into the Executive Master of Business Administration School. Wow! Hanging up, I jumped around the room for a full two minutes. Then, I crashed onto my bed, realizing I'd now have to pay the tuition, which was more than my yearly salary! And on top of that, there would be travel, accommodation, and food expenses. I decided then and there that I would make it work, no matter what.

So for the next two years, I flew to London for one weekend every month while still working full time. I managed it without a loan, but it meant sacrificing my holidays, spare time, and savings, essentially giving up all that was not strictly necessary—including even such small things like pizza dinners with my hubby. These were really tough times of barely getting by.

I remember thinking how much I wanted freedom, and wondered if it would ever be possible for me to have ALL THAT I WANT, without sacrificing so much.

On the last day of school, one of my professors said, "Now, go find yourself a mentor." I immediately thought, "But I just finished two years in this school! I don't need a mentor!" I believed I was well-equipped to go bravely into the corporate world and crush it.

I must laugh now; I was such a naïve girl! Of course, that didn't happen. After my graduation, my work colleagues congratulated me, and that was it. While I had expected something like a new contract the very day I earned my graduation certificate, nothing changed. I was perplexed. *Why?*

In the meantime, in late 2016, my husband started a personal and professional development program with Bob Proctor, who is now my own mentor, as well. But at that time, I absolutely rejected the idea! For me, the whole thing was just nice, "let's be motivated" type nonsense. I wanted facts! Tangibles.

But three weeks after starting, my hubby's professional environment, team, and opportunities changed so dramatically that I became curious. What is this stuff that can change your results in three weeks? I had spent two years working at it and hadn't even gotten a promotion! I just had to know, because he seemed to be achieving exactly what I was looking for. So, I changed my mind, and asked to be part of it.

Studying the materials, the first topic I was confronted with was goal setting. What?! In all my schooling, I had never learned how to set personal, financial, and life goals. The only goals I knew about were those your line manager sets *for* you. How much did I want to earn? I was perplexed; "I get the salary set in a contract," I thought.

**I came to understand a crucial shift in mindset:**

My salary did not come *from* my employer, but *through* my employer, and the amount I received was the amount I *thought* and *believed* I was worth, from the Universe (or God). If I wanted more, I would have to create a new belief.

*Woooow!* "Wait a sec," I thought. "I can decide I want a promotion? Higher salary?" It was time to test the theory, and guess what? A month and a half after changing that belief, I got a promotion! I was ecstatic, and more than ready to continue testing it. So, I decided I want a bigger home with more perks, and our new apartment came a couple of months later. I then yearned for another promotion, and I got it, as well. That's right—two promotions in two years! I wanted to fly business class, and I did ... six times in a row on long-haul flights.

All of the sudden, I realized I was LIVING the lifestyle I had been trying so hard to create all my life. And it seemed so easy! I was simply following exactly what my mentor advised through his program: SHIFT YOUR PARADIGM!

Of course, there were some inevitable lows. Whenever I strayed from the path, my results drifted. My finances would get low, and I'd experience difficulties.

But my biggest change—my transformation—was yet to come.

Under my mentor's guidance, it was time to *accept my true purpose and express it in constant action*. I had to stop hiding, stop being afraid, and stop minimizing myself. I had to re-create my self-image as I came to realize who I really am. I had to change my thoughts and perception *about myself*.

I had to internalize my new mission—to be an inspiring woman leader who guides others through the exact process I was learning myself: that of going full out and becoming a professional business owner! And to do that, I had to change a lot of habits, limiting beliefs, and perhaps most importantly, my self-image ... all of which I could never have done without my mentor.

Fast-forward to today—the personal transformation work I have done has finally yielded the tangible results I have always wanted: complete change, including in my finances. While all around me, people are saying, "This is a tough time; the economy is declining; there are no jobs, no salaries, no income; panic and crisis everywhere," I choose to believe in what I WANT, regardless of circumstances. I don't allow myself to get caught up in negative, depressing emotions. I choose to view now as the time people most need help with changing habitual ways of thinking that keep them stuck, so they can gain absolute clarity and faith while reaching their goals!

I persisted in stepping into my leadership, and am so happy to report that I have recently experienced my *best months ever* in terms of income AND my entire life. Through all my professional activities combined, I earned 40k U.S. dollars in two months—the equivalent of three years' earnings in my past—doing the work I love!

But the best reward of all is waking up in the morning to messages from clients like these: "I have landed my dream job! I just got the contract!" or "I have bought the car I have been dreaming about for years!" or "I earned 14k US dollars in two weeks!"

And I've just begun. I will never stop helping people get what they want, because I believe with all my heart that they *can* have it all!

That's what I want YOU, too. You have the same infinite potential that I discovered in myself.

My advice is to begin with some "baby steps" to initiate the change you seek and start the growth process.

**Here is a simple-yet-effective exercise to do so:**

Every morning, sit down and write out your answers to the following questions:

1. What are my goals that inspire me and get me going? What do I want to accomplish, to own, to be?

2. Who is the person I need to become in order to accomplish this?

3. What beliefs and habits do I need to change to make it happen?

This is something you can do today—even right now! Answering these questions will help ensure your self-image is aligned with your goals, which will increase your chances of success.

When it comes to harnessing the power of your mind, the best advice I have for you is the same that I received from my teacher: get yourself a mentor to help you work on your self-image. The magic comes in realizing who you really are, and changing your habitual thoughts, feelings, perceptions, and actions related to your self-image. This is my favorite lesson, and it made the biggest impact on my life in terms of being accountable, putting in the effort, getting the ROI, and seeing tangible results.

**You CAN Have It All!** The question is … how badly do you really want it? If you have a burning desire to achieve it (whatever that "it" might be for you), and the drive to do whatever it takes to get it, you're already on your way.

Petra Buric wears a double hat—she's a marketing expert in corporate, working in a big multinational, and she's a certified PGI consultant/coach for mindset, leadership, change management, and paradigm shifting for individuals as well as teams. After finishing her Executive MBA in Summer 2016, she started a journey of personal development and transformation, which resulted in establishing a consultancy and coaching company, Empowered Life, together with her husband Marko. Petra's purpose is to inspire and motivate people so they can discover their full potential and show them how they can start using it in practical ways to create the life and business they want and achieve permanent results in the chosen area, be it professionally or privately. You can learn more about her here: https://www.facebook.com/petra.buric.TIR/.

**Get Petra's gift to you, her workbook titled *Sweet or Strong? The Self-Image Booster,* to guide you in the next steps to take in order to change your self-image, discover your path, and create the results you truly want, here: https://hopebookseries.com/gifts/.**

# The AWE Network

The Amazing Women Entrepreneurs Network is a rapidly growing supportive community of tens of thousands of women who are inspired to take their business and life to the next level.

As you begin taking action to create and build your dream life and business, the Amazing Women Entrepreneurs Network is an invaluable resource. It's a place to come for the advice, information, and support that will make your journey efficient and fun.

**Here, you'll find all in one place the community, accountability, education, support, exposure, opportunities, resources, and inspiration you need to build a thriving business around your unique gifts!**

The Amazing Women Entrepreneurs Network takes a holistic approach to educating and empowering women to nurture each of five pillars: business, money, mind, body, and spirit. When all of these pillars are strong, a woman can thrive!

Visit amazingwomenentrepreneurs.com and discover:

- **Several gifts designed to give you expert advice on building your business,** including tips and strategies for increasing your visibility, creating a profitable, automated sales funnel, working toward financial freedom, slaying Instagram, and so much more (new gifts added often)!

- **A content-rich blog, with posts about every aspect of living your entrepreneurial dream life,** such as how to attract more clients with content you already have, what to look for in a coaching certification, how to develop new blog topics, and more.

- **eBooks, planners, journals, workbooks, and courses** designed to help you grow your business using proven step-by-step processes.

- **Opportunities to increase your exposure** through our vast network of supportive, positive women entrepreneurs.

- **And more.**

If you'd like a taste of what the Amazing Women Entrepreneurs Network can do for you, check out all the invaluable gifts at amazingwomenentrepreneursnetwork.com/free-goodies/.

If you've ever dreamed of using your business to change the world... but you've been waiting for the "right time," *Your Time Is Now* is for you!

Whether you're still in the dream phase, you want to leave the corporate world and pursue your business full time, or you want to scale your business to the next level, now is the time to take a leap of faith … and this book will provide you with tips and strategies for doing so.

You CAN design, launch, and build your dream business, starting today, no matter what your life looks like now.

You CAN use your experiences, gifts, and passions to transform people's lives.

And you CAN make great money, while living a purpose-filled life!

In this book, 22 amazing women share the inspirational, thought-provoking stories of when they realized it was time to take a leap of faith—and how they took action to start or scale their businesses and live their dreams.

You'll discover how they transformed their mindsets to leverage their success, the practical steps they took to go from employee to entrepreneur, the strategies they used to take their businesses to the next level, and where they found the courage to go for it.

You'll also find exercises and practical action steps to apply these hard-earned lessons to your own life, so you can finally start making your vision a reality.

If you've ever dreamed of using your own business to change the world …

Your time is now.

Order your copy today, and become inspired to take action and change the world.

**Go here to get your copy: https://hopebookseries.com.**


**From hopeless, lost, and desperate for answers to resilient, happy, and healthy!**

A serious health condition can have a significant impact on your life.

If you're dealing with one, you've probably found yourself unable to do the things you enjoy with the people you love. Maybe you've struggled to work the way you want to, as well.

And maybe, you've wondered if your life will ever be "normal" again, as you go through a gauntlet of emotions: fear, stress, frustration, despair.

There *is* good news, even if you feel like healing is impossible.

**You can get better.**

In *Oh My Health … There Is Hope*, 17 people share their true stories of overcoming serious health conditions and reclaiming their lives.

From diagnoses of Epstein Barr virus to obsessive-compulsive disorder and chronic stress to chronic pain, the contributors to this heartfelt book felt lost and hopeless, too. They searched for answers, and didn't find them … at first.

Although their stories are unique, there's one common thread: they didn't give up. They searched tirelessly for answers until they were finally able to heal.

Reading *Oh My Health* will give you a renewed sense of hope and determination as you realize that you're *not* alone—and more importantly, that you can find a solution to your current health crisis.

When you do, you'll get your life back!

Each contributor shares a personal story of triumph, as well as exercises and action steps to begin your journey to better health.

If you're ready to find hope again, order your copy today, and become inspired to take action and reclaim your health and life.

**Go here to get your copy:** <u>https://hopebookseries.com/</u>.

# Want to co-author one of our books?

If you want to bring your brand or movement into the world in a BIG Way, then the Hope Book Series is for you!

The Hope Book Series is for anyone looking to bring their products, brand, or service into the world with integrity and power that lights up your life. It's about growing a business you are deeply in love with, making an incredible living *and* impact as you help millions around the globe.

Getting yourself or your brand "omnipresent" is the answer to consistency and profits. Because when it comes to success, it's NOT who you know—it's WHO KNOWS YOU!

We too are on a mission to create a movement of success for women around the world, so they can live a life they love and have a business that provides them the freedom lifestyle they deserve.

The Amazing Women Entrepreneurs Network believes it takes five pillars to THRIVE. Those pillars are Business, Wealth, Mind, Body, and Spirit. When one pillar is broken, it affects the others.

We aim to educate and empower women about taking a holistic approach to enjoying a thriving life.

If you love the "Chicken Soup for the Soul" inspirational books, then you will love our Hope Book Series for women.

Right now, we are accepting co-author applications for up-coming anthologies in the "Hope Book Series." (Topics include business, money, health, spirituality, career, life, mindset, over-coming trauma, transformation, and so on.)

**To learn more about becoming a contributor, visit** www.hopebookseries.com/coauthor**.**

Check out the Amazing Women of Influence Podcast!

Hosted by Serena Carcasole. Real Stories, tools, and strategic tips for your life and business. Listen to courageous conversations and valuable tips and takeaways to create the business and life of your dreams. https://www.amazingwomenofinfluence.com

## Amazing Women Club

www.amazingwomen.club

**Global Business Networking and Visibility Club for Women**

Tired of feeling like a needle in a haystack? Ready to finally be seen and heard by the right people, so you can grow your business, impact, and profits?

You CAN get visible, uplift others, and build an audience of raving superfans who can't wait to buy your next offer!

Join the **Amazing Women Club,** and step into an elite virtual network of hand-picked, high-powered women business owners dedicated to mutual growth. When you do, you'll take your business to a new level, thanks to a new, exciting energy that produces results.

If you want leads who are ready to buy (and who turn into raving superfans after that first purchase), the income that follows, and the knowledge that you're making a difference on a massive scale—all without working 24/7, then **follow this link to learn more about the Amazing Women Club:** https://www.amazingwomen.club.

# Thriving Women Magazine

If you're a woman entrepreneur on a mission to thrive—not just in business, but personally, too—then you'll definitely want to read **Thriving Women Magazine**! Every issue is full of powerful content that will guide you in upleveling every aspect of your life.

Covering every topic imaginable when it comes to thriving— human connection, mindset, productivity, branding, marketing, stress management, growing your audience, mental health, profits, and more—*Thriving Women Magazine* is an unparalleled resource for the entrepreneur looking to flourish.

**Learn more about the free digital *Thriving Women Magazine* here: http://www.thrivingwomenmag.com.**

Made in the USA
Coppell, TX
15 July 2021